HYMNS WE LOVE TO SING

HYMNS WE LOVE TO SING

Geneva Press
Louisville, Kentucky

*Geneva Press wishes to thank
Martha Gillis, the Rev. Paul Detterman, and Debbie Dierks
for selecting the hymns for this book.*

© 2001 Geneva Press

All rights reserved. No part of this book may be reproduced or transmitted in any form or by any means, electronic or mechanical, including photocopying, recording, or by any information storage or retrieval system, without permission in writing from the publisher. For information, address Geneva Press, 100 Witherspoon Street, Louisville, Kentucky 40202-1396.

The publisher is grateful to all who have granted permission to use songs they control. Individual notice of such permission is given below the songs. Every effort has been made to determine whether texts and music are under copyright. If through an oversight any copyrighted material has been used without permission, and the publisher is notified of this, acknowledgment will be made in future printings.

Book design by A-R Editions, Inc.
Hard Edition Cover design by Kathy York
Paper Edition Cover design by Lisa Buckley

First edition
Published by Geneva Press
Louisville, Kentucky

This book is printed on acid-free paper that meets the American National Standards Institute Z39.48 standard. ∞

PRINTED IN THE UNITED STATES OF AMERICA
01 02 03 04 05 06 07 08 09 10 — 10 9 8 7 6 5 4 3 2 1

ISBN 0-664-50176-1 (Hard)
ISBN 0-664-50187-7 (Paper)

CONTENTS AND ORGANIZATION OF HYMNS

	Page
Foreword	7
HYMNS	Hymn
CHRISTIAN YEAR	
Advent	1
Christmas	2
Epiphany	5
Lent	6
Holy Week	8
Trinity Sunday	12
Christ the King	14
PSALMS	
Psalm 23	17
TOPICAL HYMNS	
God	18
Jesus Christ	28
Holy Spirit	46
Holy Scripture	50
Life in Christ	53
Church	87
Morning and Opening Hymns	95
Sacraments	103
Ordination and Confirmation	106
Funeral	107
Evening Hymns	112
Any Occasion	114
	Page
Index of First Lines and Common Titles	217

FOREWORD

"Faith is meant to be sung, and hymns are for the singing of it. Some say that hymns are a greater influence on one's personal theology even than scripture or teaching or preaching or family or friends. I believe this is also true of the influence of hymns on our collective theology as part of the Judeo-Christian tradition, and especially the Reformed tradition. With psalms and chants, chorales and canons, spirituals and choruses, hymns and folk songs, we have sung our faith. Words that are sung, especially if they are sung repeatedly and enthusiastically, work their way into our subconscious and shape us in subtle ways, as well as giving us words and phrases that come quickly to mind when we ponder or articulate our faith."

Thus began *A Singing Faith*, my first real book of hymns, new words to mostly familiar tunes. It still rings true.

That being said, the hymns selected for this collection represent the "good old hymns" in the minds of the selectors. Any individual person or group would eliminate some of these and add others because "favorites" are specific to individuals.

On seeing the list for the first time, I noticed that many of these hymns date from the mid-nineteenth century to the first quarter of the twentieth century. What that probably means is that these hymns are primarily the favorites of people born from about 1920–1950 or, perhaps more likely, the favorites of their parents and grandparents. That is not to discredit them but rather to point out that they are favorites because they are the hymns we "grew up on." What makes them favorites are the memories and the people we associate with them.

As one member of the committee who worked for five years on *The Presbyterian Hymnal: Hymns, Psalms, and Spiritual Songs* (Westminster/John Knox Press, 1990), I need to say that most of the hymns in this present collection were considered for inclusion in that volume. Our task was to compile a hymnbook for contemporary use that was "in inclusive language" and "representative of the diversity of the church." I affirm the General Assembly's commission to that committee and also the guidelines developed by the committee. On the other hand, this volume of old favorites illustrates clearly that inclusion or exclusion in a hymnal does not mean the life or death of a particular hymn. We are not forbidden from singing hymns that are meaningful in our faith!

Along with others, I enjoy singing the hymns of my childhood. In general, the tunes are singable, in an easy range for most voices, with predictable rhythms. And of course, we all know an amazing number by heart. The words more than the music reflect the way other generations expressed their faith. Because former manners of speech are sometimes not my way of expressing my faith, I am grateful that there are new hymns to sing in addition to old favorites. Words from any period of hymnody may become obsolete or change their meaning radically or subtly. One way to be realistic about this fact is to recognize that the church's music and hymns evolve over time, sometimes to our delight, sometimes to our distress.

An interesting challenge to, and yet corroboration of, the idea of evolving hymnody can be found in African-American spirituals and folk songs. Because these forms of faith songs grew out of daily experience, were learned orally, and were often not written down for generations, they grew and changed in different ways. The meaning of spirituals often was deliberately hidden to protect slaves who were singing, and today the hidden meaning and the words themselves might change to meet a new difficulty or to give new information. "Steal away, steal away, steal away to Jesus" was a call to a worship service, or it might signal escape to freedom in this life as well as to heaven. Folk hymns of other traditions also give faithful believers hope of a better life, hereafter if not right away. "I'll Fly Away" is one example.

So, here is a *new* collection of *old* favorites. Sing them with enthusiasm and faith. I hope our collective faith is also expressed in the language of our day because our God is a God of yesterday, today, and tomorrow, going on before us giving light and music to all our journeys.

Jane Parker Huber

ADVENT

Lift Up Your Heads, Ye Mighty Gates

TRURO L.M.

Georg Weissel, 1642
trans. Catherine Winkworth, 1855

Thomas Williams, 1789
harm. Lowell Mason (1792–1872)

1

1. Lift up your heads, ye might-y gates, Be-hold, the King of glo-ry waits; The King of kings is draw-ing near; The Sav-ior of the world is here!
2. Fling wide the port-als of your heart; Make it a tem-ple, set a-part From earth-ly use for heaven's em-ploy, A-dorned with prayer, and love, and joy.
3. Re-deem-er, come! I o-pen wide My heart to Thee; here, Lord, a-bide. Let me Thy in-ner pres-ence feel; Thy grace and love in me re-veal.

CHRISTMAS

2 Go, Tell It on the Mountain
GO TELL IT   7.6.7.6 with Refrain

stanzas, John W. Work II (1872–1925)

African-American spiritual
arr. John W. Work III, 1940
harm. and adapt. Melva Wilson Costen, 1987

Refrain

Go, tell it on the moun - tain, O-ver the hills, and ev - ery-where;

Fine

Go, tell it on the moun - tain That Je - sus Christ is born!

1. While shep-herds kept their watch-ing O'er si - lent flocks by night,
2. The shep-herds feared and trem-bled When lo! a - bove the earth,
3. Down in a low - ly man - ger The hum-ble Christ was born,

D.C.

Be - hold through-out the heav-ens There shone a ho - ly light.
Rang out the an - gel cho - rus That hailed our Sav - ior's birth.
And God sent us sal - va - tion That bless - ed Christ-mas morn.

Music: harmonization and adaptation © 1989 by Melva Wilson Costen. All rights reserved. Used by permission.

CHRISTMAS

Lo, How a Rose E'er Blooming

ES IST EIN' ROS'   7.6.7.6.6.7.6

3

German carol, 15th century
trans. Theodore Baker (1851–1934)
alt. *Rejoice in the Lord,* 1985

Alte Catholische Geistliche Kirchengesäng, Cologne, 1599
arr. Michael Praetorius, 1609

1. Lo, how a rose e'er bloom-ing From ten-der stem hath sprung,
Of Jes-se's lin-eage com-ing, By faith-ful proph-ets sung.
It came a flower-et bright, A-mid the cold of win-ter,
When half spent was the night.

2. I-sa-iah 'twas fore-told it, The rose I have in mind,
With Mar-y we be-hold it, The vir-gin moth-er kind.
To show God's love a-right She bore for us a Sav-ior
When half spent was the night.

(was the)

CHRISTMAS

4 Rise Up, Shepherd, and Follow

African-American spiritual · African-American spiritual

1. There's a star in the East on Christmas morn,
2. If you take good heed to the angel's words,

Rise up, shepherd, and follow;

It will lead to the place where the Christ was born,
You'll forget your flocks, you'll forget your herds,

Rise up, shepherd, and follow.

Refrain
Follow, follow, Rise up, shepherd, and follow,
Follow the Star of Bethlehem, Rise up, shepherd, and follow.

EPIPHANY

As with Gladness Men of Old

DIX 7.7.7.7.7.7

5

William Chatterton Dix, c. 1858

Conrad Kocher, 1838
abr. William Henry Monk, 1861
harm. *The English Hymnal,* 1906

1. As with glad-ness men of old Did the guid-ing star be-hold;
2. As with joy-ful steps they sped To that low-ly man-ger bed,
3. As they of-fered gifts most rare At that man-ger rude and bare,
4. Ho-ly Je-sus, ev-ery day Keep us in the nar-row way;

As with joy they hailed its light, Lead-ing on-ward, beam-ing bright;
There to bend the knee be-fore Him whom heaven and earth a-dore;
So may we with ho-ly joy, Pure and free from sin's al-loy,
And, when earth-ly things are past, Bring our ran-somed souls at last

So, most gra-cious Lord, may we Ev-er-more be led to Thee.
So may we with will-ing feet Ev-er seek Thy mer-cy seat.
All our cost-liest treas-ures bring, Christ, to Thee, our heaven-ly King.
Where they need no star to guide, Where no clouds Thy glo-ry hide.

LENT

6 Jesus Walked This Lonesome Valley
LONESOME VALLEY 8.8.10.8

American spiritual American spiritual

1. Jesus walked this lonesome valley; He had to walk it by Himself; Oh, nobody else could walk it for Him; He had to walk it by Himself.
2. We must walk this lonesome valley; We have to walk it by ourselves; Oh, nobody else can walk it for us; We have to walk it by ourselves.
3. You must go and stand your trial; You have to stand it by yourself; Oh, nobody else can stand it for you; You have to stand it by yourself.

Down at the Cross

LENT 7

Elisha A. Hoffman (1839–1929), alt.

1. Down at the cross where my Sav-ior died, Down where for cleans-ing from sin I cried, There to my heart was the blood ap-plied—
2. I am so won-drous-ly saved from sin, Je-sus so sweet-ly a-bides with-in; There at the cross where Christ took me in—
3. O pre-cious foun-tain that saves from sin, I am so glad I have en-tered in; There Je-sus saves me and keeps me clean—
4. Come to this foun-tain so rich and sweet, Cast your poor soul at the Sav-ior's feet; Plunge in to-day and be made com-plete—

Refrain
Glo-ry to Christ's name. Glo-ry to Christ's name, Glo-ry to Christ's name; There to my heart was the blood ap-plied; Glo-ry to Christ's name.

HOLY WEEK

8. Beneath the Cross of Jesus
ST. CHRISTOPHER 7.6.8.6.8.6.8.6

Elizabeth Cecilia Douglas Clephane, 1868 — Frederick Charles Maker, 1881

1. Beneath the cross of Jesus I fain would take my stand,
The shadow of a mighty rock Within a weary land;
A home within the wilderness, A rest upon the way,
From the burning of the noontide heat, And the burden of the day.

2. Upon the cross of Jesus Mine eye at times can see
The very dying form of One Who suffered there for me:
And from my stricken heart with tears Two wonders I confess:
The wonders of redeeming love And my unworthiness.

Ah, Holy Jesus

HERZLIEBSTER JESU 11.11.11.5

HOLY WEEK

9

Johann Heermann, 1630
trans. Robert Bridges, 1899
alt. *Psalter Hymnal*, 1987

Johann Crüger, 1640

1. Ah, holy Jesus, how have You offended, That mortal judgment has on You descended? By foes derided, by Your own rejected, O most afflicted!
2. Who was the guilty? Who brought this upon You? It is my treason, Lord, that has undone You. 'Twas I, Lord Jesus, I it was denied You; I crucified You.
3. For me, dear Jesus, was Your incarnation, Your mortal sorrow, and Your life's oblation, Your death of anguish and Your bitter passion, For my salvation.
4. Therefore, dear Jesus, since I cannot pay You, I do adore You, and will ever praise You, Think on Your pity and Your love unswerving, Not my deserving.

HOLY WEEK

10 When I Survey the Wondrous Cross
ROCKINGHAM   L.M.

Isaac Watts, 1707

Second Supplement to Psalmody in Miniature, 1783
harm. Edward Miller, 1790

1. When I survey the wondrous cross On which the Prince of glory died, My richest gain I count but loss, And pour contempt on all my pride.
2. Forbid it, Lord, that I should boast, Save in the death of Christ my God; All the vain things that charm me most, I sacrifice them to His blood.
3. See, from His head, His hands, His feet, Sorrow and love flow mingled down; Did e'er such love and sorrow meet, Or thorns compose so rich a crown?
4. Were the whole realm of nature mine, That were a present far too small; Love so amazing, so divine, Demands my soul, my life, my all.

HOLY WEEK

Were You There?

WERE YOU THERE Irregular

African-American spiritual

African-American spiritual
arr. Melva Wilson Costen, 1987

11

1. Were you there when they cru - ci - fied my Lord? _____
2. Were you there when they nailed Him to the tree? _____
3. Were you there when they pierced Him in the side? _____
4. Were you there when they laid Him in the tomb? _____

(Were you there?)

Were you there when they cru - ci - fied my Lord?
Were you there when they nailed Him to the tree?
Were you there when they pierced Him in the side?
Were you there when they laid Him in the tomb?

Oh!

Some-times it caus-es me to trem-ble, trem-ble, trem-ble.

Were you there when they cru - ci - fied my Lord? _____
Were you there when they nailed Him to the tree? _____
Were you there when they pierced Him in the side? _____
Were you there when they laid Him in the tomb? _____

(Were you there?)

Music: arrangements © 1990 Melva Wilson Casten. All rights reserved. Used by permission.

TRINITY SUNDAY

12 Holy, Holy, Holy! Lord God Almighty!
NICAEA 11.12.12.10

Reginald Heber (1783–1826)
as in *Hymns Written and Adapted*, 1827, alt.

John Bacchus Dykes, 1861
desc. David McKinley Williams, 1948

4. Ho — — — — — ly,

1. Lord God Almighty!
2. Holy, holy, holy! all the saints adore Thee,
3. Holy, holy, holy! though the darkness hide Thee,
4. Lord God Almighty!

Ho — — — — — ly,

Early in the morning our song shall rise to Thee;
Casting down their golden crowns around the glassy sea;
Though the eye of sinfulness Thy glory may not see;
All Thy works shall praise Thy name, in earth and sky and sea;

Music: descant © 1948 (renewed) The H.W. Gray Company. All rights administered by Warner Bros. Publications U.S. Inc. All rights reserved.

TRINITY SUNDAY

Holy, holy, holy! merciful and mighty!
Cherubim and seraphim falling down before Thee,
Only Thou art holy; there is none beside Thee
Holy, holy, holy! merciful and mighty!

God in three Persons, blessed Trinity!
Who wert, and art, and evermore shalt be.
Perfect in power, in love and purity.
God in three Persons, blessed Trinity!

TRINITY SUNDAY

13 Come, Thou Almighty King
ITALIAN HYMN 6.6.4.6.6.6.4

Collection of Hymns for Social Worship, 1757, alt. Felice de Giardini, 1769

1. Come, Thou Almighty King, Help us Thy name to sing, Help us to praise: Father, all-glorious, O'er all victorious, Come, and reign over us, Ancient of Days.
2. Come, Thou Incarnate Word, Gird on Thy mighty sword, Our prayer attend: Come, and Thy people bless, And give Thy word success; Spirit of holiness, On us descend.
3. Come, Holy Comforter, Thy sacred witness bear In this glad hour: Thou who almighty art, Now rule in every heart, And ne'er from us depart, Spirit of power.
4. To Thee, great One in Three, The highest praises be, Hence evermore! Thy sovereign majesty May we in glory see, And to eternity Love and adore.

CHRIST THE KING

All Hail the Power of Jesus' Name!   14
CORONATION   8.6.8.6.8.6

stanzas 1–3, Edward Perronet, 1779, 1780
stanzas 2–3, alt. John Rippon, 1787
stanza 4, John Rippon, 1787

Oliver Holden, 1793
desc. Michael E. Young, 1979

Descant
4. Oh, that with yon-der sa-cred throng We at His feet may fall!

1. All hail the power of Je-sus' name! Let an-gels pros-trate fall;
2. Ye cho-sen seed of Is-rael's race, Ye ran-somed from the fall,
3. Let ev-ery kin-dred, ev-ery tribe, On this ter-res-trial ball,
4. Oh, that with yon-der sa-cred throng We at His feet may fall!

We'll join the song And crown Him Lord of all!

Bring forth the roy-al di-a-dem,
Hail Him who saves you by His grace,
To Him all maj-es-ty as-cribe,
We'll join the ev-er-last-ing song

And crown Him Lord of all!

We'll join the song And crown Him Lord of all!

Bring forth the roy-al di-a-dem,
Hail Him who saves you by His grace,
To Him all maj-es-ty as-cribe,
We'll join the ev-er-last-ing song

And crown Him Lord of all!

Music: descant copyright © 1979 by G.I.A. Publications, Inc., Chicago, Illinois. All rights reserved.

CHRIST THE KING

15 Come, Christians, Join to Sing
MADRID 6.6.6.6.D

Christian Henry Bateman, 1843

Spanish folk melody
arr. Benjamin Carr, 1824
harm. David Evans, 1927

1. Come, Christians, join to sing Loud praise to Christ our King; Let all, with heart and voice, Before His throne rejoice; Praise is His gracious choice: Alleluia! Amen!
2. Come, lift your hearts on high; Let praises fill the sky; Alleluia! Amen! He is our guide and friend; To us He'll condescend; His love shall never end; Alleluia! Amen!
3. Praise yet our Christ again; Life shall not end the strain; On heaven's blissful shore His goodness we'll adore, Singing forevermore, "Alleluia! Amen!"

Harmonization: David Evans (1872–1958) from *The Revised Church Hymnary* © Oxford University Press 1927. Used by permission. All rights reserved.

CHRIST THE KING

Rejoice, the Lord Is King

16

DARWALL'S 148TH 6.6.6.6.8.8

Charles Wesley, 1746

John Darwall, 1770
desc. Sidney Hugo Nicholson (1875–1947)

Descant

3. Re-joice in glo-rious hope! For Christ, the Judge, shall come

1. Re-joice, the Lord is King! Your Lord and King a-dore!
2. God's king-dom can-not fail, Christ rules o'er earth and heaven;
3. Re-joice in glo-rious hope! For Christ, the Judge, shall come

To glo-ri-fy the saints For their e-ter-nal home:

Re-joice, give thanks, and sing, And tri-umph ev-er-more:
The keys of death and hell Are to our Je-sus given:
To glo-ri-fy the saints For their e-ter-nal home:

Lift up your heart, lift up your voice! Re-joice, a-gain I say, re-joice!

Lift up your heart, lift up your voice! Re-joice, a-gain I say, re-joice!

Note: this tune in a higher key and without descant, *The Presbyterian Hymnal* # 430

Music: descant © by Hope Publishing Co., Carol Stream, IL 60188. All rights reserved. Used by permission.

PSALM 23

17 The Lord's My Shepherd, I'll Not Want
CRIMOND C.M.

Scottish Psalter, 1650

Jessie Seymour Irvine, 1872
harm. T.C.L. Pritchard, 1929

1. The Lord's my Shepherd, I'll not want;
   He makes me down to lie
   In pastures green; He leadeth me
   The quiet waters by.

2. My soul He doth restore again;
   And me to walk doth make
   Within the paths of righteousness,
   E'en for His own name's sake.

3. Yea, though I walk in death's dark vale,
   Yet will I fear none ill;
   For Thou art with me; and Thy rod
   And staff me comfort still.

4. My table Thou hast furnished
   In presence of my foes;
   My head Thou dost with oil anoint,
   And my cup o'erflows.

5. Goodness and mercy all my life
   Shall surely follow me;
   And in God's house forevermore
   My dwelling place shall be.

Music: harmonization from *The Scottish Psalter*, 1929. Used by permission of Oxford University Press.

GOD

God Moves in a Mysterious Way

DUNDEE C.M.

18

William Cowper, 1774 — *Scottish Psalter, 1615*

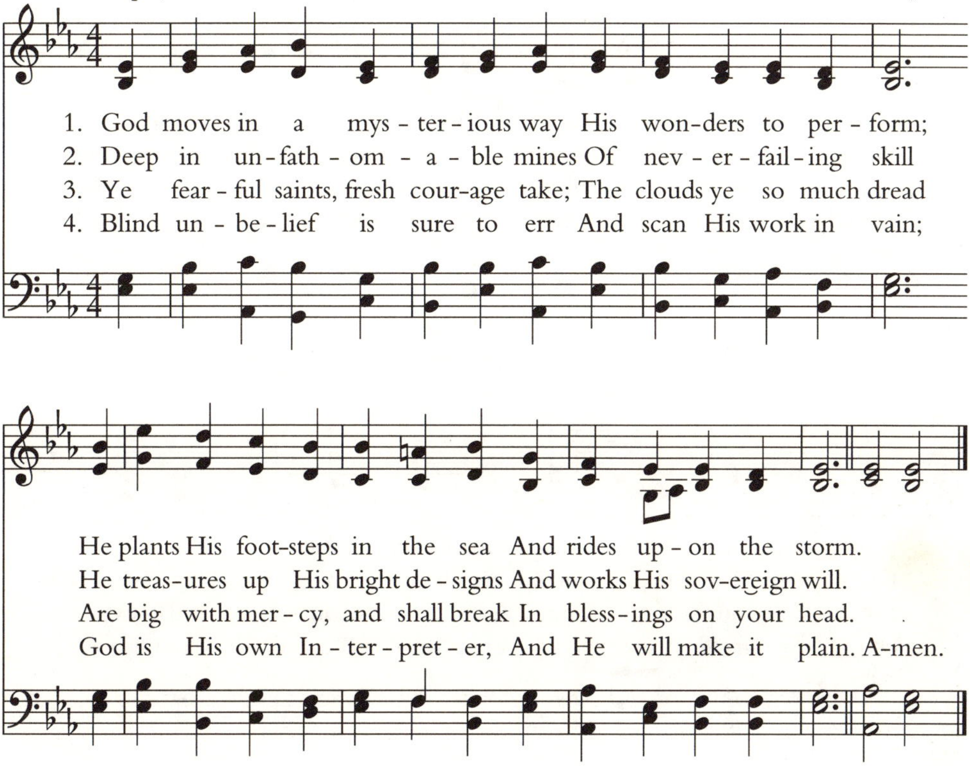

1. God moves in a mysterious way His wonders to perform;
   He plants His footsteps in the sea And rides upon the storm.
2. Deep in unfathomable mines Of never-failing skill
   He treasures up His bright designs And works His sovereign will.
3. Ye fearful saints, fresh courage take; The clouds ye so much dread
   Are big with mercy, and shall break In blessings on your head.
4. Blind unbelief is sure to err And scan His work in vain;
   God is His own Interpreter, And He will make it plain. A-men.

Alternative Accompaniment

Melody in the Tenor — arr. by Thomas Ravenscroft, 1621

Note: This alternative arrangement may be used for one or more stanzas, the congregation singing the melody only.

GOD

19 He Leadeth Me: O Blessed Thought
HE LEADETH ME   L.M. with Refrain

Joseph H. Gilmore, 1862 (Ps. 23)   William B. Bradbury, 1864

1. He lead-eth me: O bless-ed thought! O words with heaven-ly com-fort fraught! What-e'er I do, wher-e'er I be, Still 'tis God's hand that lead-eth me.
2. Some-times 'mid scenes of deep-est gloom, Some-times where E-den's bow-ers bloom, By wa-ters still, o'er trou-bled sea, Still 'tis His hand that lead-eth me.
3. Lord, I would place my hand in Thine, Nor ev-er mur-mur nor re-pine; Con-tent, what-ev-er lot I see, Since 'tis my God that lead-eth me.
4. And when my task on earth is done, When by thy grace the vic-tory's won, E'en death's cold wave I will not flee, Since God through Jor-dan lead-eth me.

GOD

Refrain

He lead-eth me, He lead-eth me, By His own hand He lead-eth me; His faith-ful fol-lower I would be, For by His hand He lead-eth me.

GOD

20 God Will Take Care of You

MARTIN C.M. with Refrain

Civilla D. Martin, 1904
W. Stillman Martin, 1905

1. Be not dismayed what-e'er betide, Beneath His wings of love abide,
2. Through days of toil when heart doth fail, When dangers fierce your path assail,
3. All you may need He will provide, Nothing you ask will be denied;
4. No matter what may be the test, Lean, weary one, upon His breast;

God will take care of you; God will take care of you.

Refrain

God will take care of you, Through every day, o'er all the way; He will take care of you, God will take care of you.

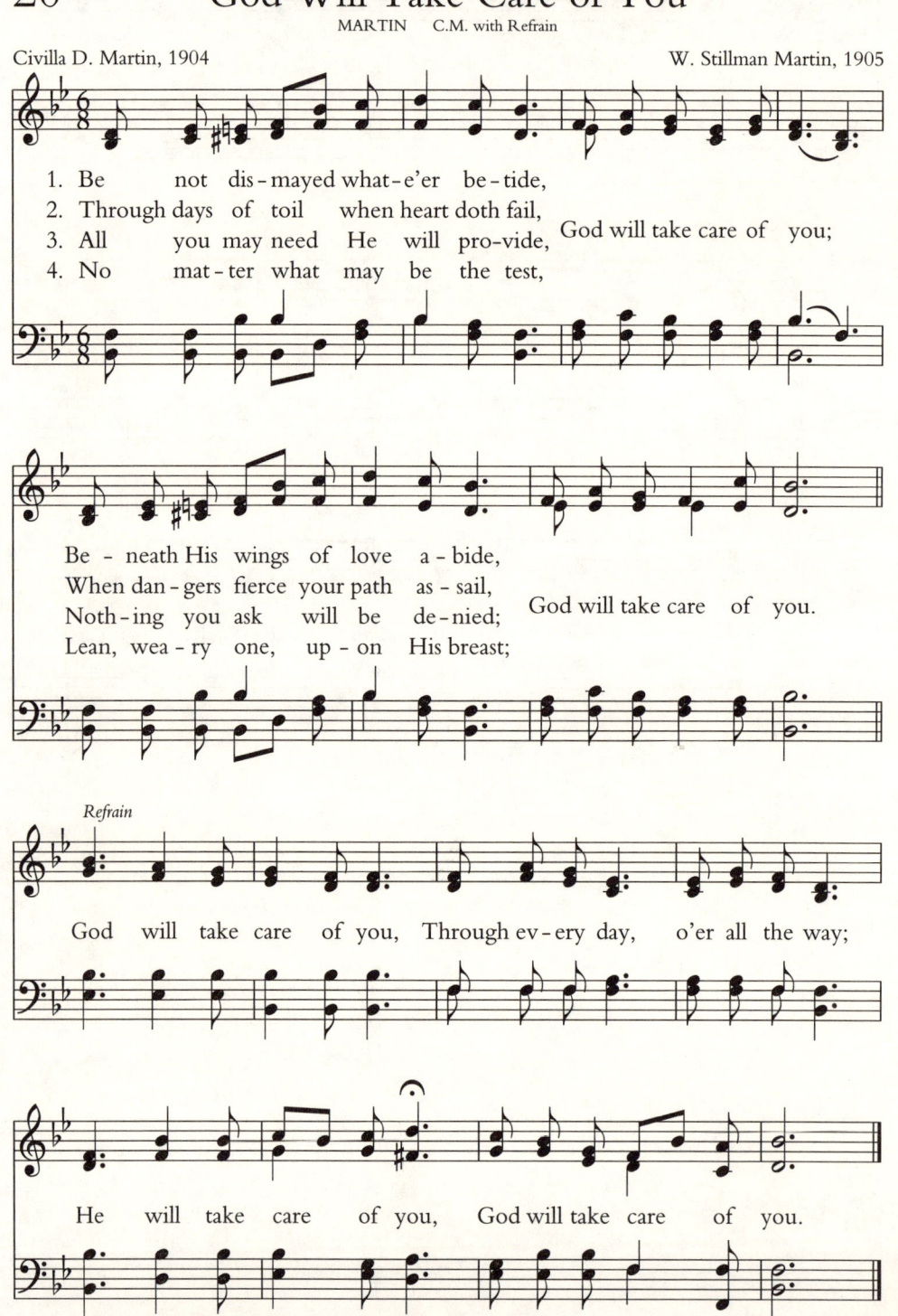

Immortal, Invisible, God Only Wise

ST. DENIO 11.11.11.11

Walter Chalmers Smith, 1867; alt. 1987

Welsh folk melody
adapted in *Caniadau y Cyssegr*, 1839

1. Immortal, invisible, God only wise,
In light inaccessible hid from our eyes,
Most blessed, most glorious, the Ancient of Days,
Almighty, victorious, Thy great name we praise.

2. Unresting, unhasting, and silent as light,
Nor wanting, nor wasting, Thou rulest in might;
Thy justice like mountains high soaring above
Thy clouds, which are fountains of goodness and love.

3. To all, life Thou givest, to both great and small;
In all life Thou livest, the true life of all;
We blossom and flourish like leaves on the tree,
Then wither and perish; but naught changeth Thee.

4. Thou reignest in glory, Thou rulest in light;
Thine angels adore Thee, all veiling their sight;
All praise we would render; oh, help us to see
'Tis only the splendor of light hideth Thee!

GOD

22 Great Is Thy Faithfulness
FAITHFULNESS 11.10.11.10 with Refrain

Thomas Obediah Chisholm, 1923 William Marion Runyan, 1923

1. *Great is Thy faithfulness, O God my Father;
2. Summer and winter, and springtime and harvest,
3. Pardon for sin and a peace that endureth,

There is no shadow of turning with Thee;
Sun, moon, and stars in their courses above
Thine own dear presence to cheer and to guide;

Thou changest not, Thy compassions they fail not;
Join with all nature in manifold witness
Strength for today and bright hope for tomorrow,

As Thou hast been, Thou forever wilt be.
To Thy great faithfulness, mercy, and love.
Blessings all mine, with ten thousand beside!

*Or "Great is Thy faithfulness, O God, Creator."

Words and Music: © 1923, renewed 1951 by Hope Publishing Co., Carol Stream, IL 60188. All rights reserved. Used by permission.

Refrain
Great is Thy faith-ful-ness! Great is Thy faith-ful-ness!
Morn-ing by morn-ing new mer-cies I see;
All I have need-ed Thy hand hath pro-vid-ed;
Great is Thy faith-ful-ness, Lord, un-to me!

GOD

23. O God of Bethel, by Whose Hand
DUNDEE C.M.

Philip Doddridge (1702–1751)
John Logan, 1781, alt.
Scottish Psalter, 1615

1. O God of Bethel, by Whose hand
Thy people still are fed,
Who through this weary pilgrimage
Hast all Thy servants led:

2. Our vows, our prayers, we now present
Before Thy throne of grace;
God of past ages, be the God
Of each succeeding race.

3. Through each perplexing path of life
Our wandering footsteps guide;
Give us each day our daily bread,
And raiment fit provide.

4. Oh, spread Thy covering wings around
Till all our wanderings cease,
And at our God's beloved abode
Our souls arrive in peace.

GOD

Amazing Grace, How Sweet the Sound   24
AMAZING GRACE   C.M.

stanzas 1–4, John Newton, 1779
stanza 5, *A Collection of Sacred Ballads*, 1790

Virginia Harmony, 1831
arr. Edwin O. Excell, 1900

1. A-maz-ing grace, how sweet the sound, That saved a wretch like me!
2. 'Twas grace that taught my heart to fear, And grace my fears re-lieved;
3. Through man-y dan-gers, toils, and snares I have al-read-y come;
4. The Lord has prom-ised good to me. His word my hope se-cures.

I once was lost, but now am found, Was blind, but now I see.
How pre-cious did that grace ap-pear The hour I first be-lieved!
'Tis grace has brought me safe thus far, And grace will lead me home.
He will my shield and por-tion be As long as life en-dures.

5. When we've been there ten thousand years,
Bright shining as the sun,
We've no less days to sing God's praise
Than when we'd first begun.

Choctaw
Shilombish holitopa ma!
Ishmminti pulla cha
Hatak ilbusha pia ha
Is pi yukpalashke

Kiowa
Daw k'ee da ha dawtsahy he tsow'haw
Daw k'ee da ha dawtsahy hee.
Bay dawtsahy taw, gaw aym ow thah t'aw,
Daw k'ee da ha dawtsahy h'ee.

Cherokee
Ooh nay thla nah, hee oo way gee'.
E gah gwoo yah hay ee.
Naw gwoo joe sah, we you low say,
E gah gwoo yah ho nah.

Creek
Po ya fek cha he thlat ah tet
Ah non ah cha pa kas
Cha fee kee o funnan la kus
Um e ha ta la yus.

Navaho
Nizhóníígo joobá diitś á
Yisdáshíítinigíí,
Lah yóóiiyá, k'ad shénáhoosdzin,
Doo eesh'íí da ńt'éé.

Text: phonetic transcription Cherokee, Kiowa, Creek, and Choctaw: Oklahoma Indian Missionary Conference; Navaho: phonetic transcription by Albert Tsosie.

GOD

25 Guide Me, O Thou Great Jehovah
CWM RHONDDA 8.7.8.7.8.7.7

William Williams, 1745
stanza 1 trans. Peter Williams, 1771
stanzas 2–3 trans. William Williams, 1772

John Hughes, 1907

1. Guide me, O Thou great Jehovah, Pilgrim through this barren land; I am weak, but Thou art mighty, Hold me with Thy powerful hand; Bread of heaven, bread of heaven, Feed me till I want no more, Feed me till I want no more.
2. Open now the crystal fountain, Whence the healing stream doth flow; Let the fire and cloudy pillar Lead me all my journey through; Strong deliverer, strong deliverer, Be Thou still my strength and shield, Be Thou still my strength and shield.
3. When I tread the verge of Jordan, Bid my anxious fears subside; Death of death, and hell's destruction, Land me safe on Canaan's side; Songs of praises, songs of praises I will ever give to Thee, I will ever give to Thee.

If Thou But Trust in God to Guide Thee   26
WER NUR DEN LIEBEN GOTT   9.8.9.8.8.8

Georg Neumark, 1657
trans. Catherine Winkworth, 1855, 1863; alt. 1987

Georg Neumark, 1657

1. If thou but trust in God to guide thee, With hopeful heart through all thy ways, God will give strength, whate'er betide thee, To bear thee through the evil days. Who trusts in God's unchanging love Builds on the rock that nought can move.

2. Only be still, and wait God's leisure In cheerful hope, with heart content To take whate'er thy Keeper's pleasure And all-discerning love hath sent. No doubt our inmost wants are clear To One who holds us always dear.

3. Sing, pray, and swerve not from God's ways, But do thine own part faithfully; Trust the rich promises of grace, So shall they be fulfilled in thee. God never yet forsook at need The soul secured by trust indeed.

GOD

27 I Sing the Mighty Power of God
ELLACOMBE C.M.D

Isaac Watts, 1715, alt.   Gesangbuch der Herzogl. Wirtembergischen Katholischen Hofkapelle, 1784; alt. 1868

1. I sing the might-y power of God That made the moun-tains rise;
That spread the flow-ing seas a-broad And built the loft-y skies.
I sing the wis-dom that or-dained The sun to rule the day;
The moon shines full at God's com-mand, And all the stars o-bey.

2. I sing the good-ness of the Lord That filled the earth with food;
God formed the crea-tures with a word And then pro-nounced them good.
Lord, how Thy won-ders are dis-played Wher-e'er I turn my eyes
If I sur-vey the ground I tread Or gaze up-on the skies!

3. There's not a plant or flower be-low But makes Thy glo-ries known;
And clouds a-rise, and tem-pests blow, By or-der from Thy throne;
While all that bor-rows life from Thee Is ev-er in Thy care,
And ev-ery-where that we can be Thou, God, art pres-ent there.

Alternate tune: FOREST GREEN, *The Presbyterian Hymnal* # 292

JESUS CHRIST

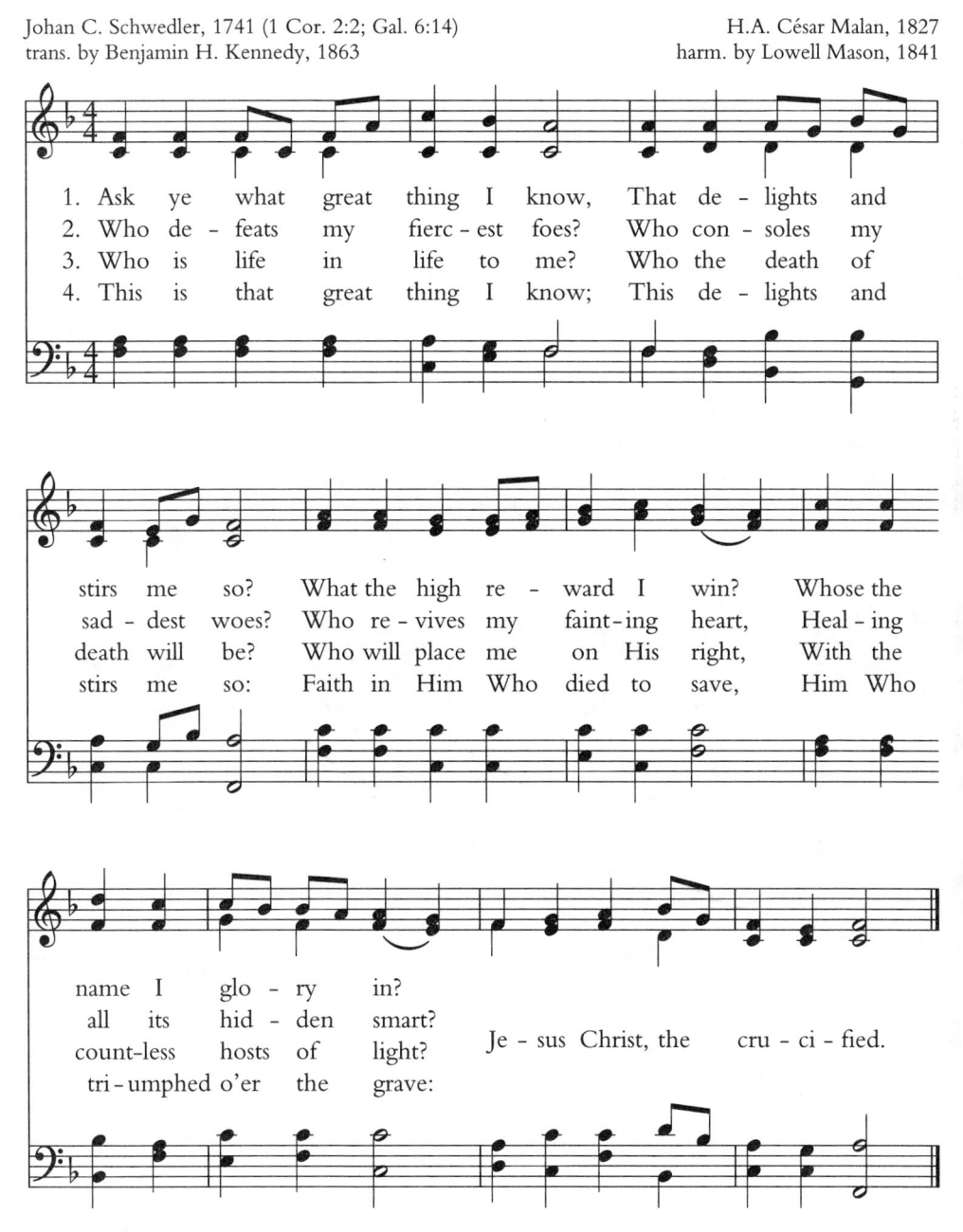

Ask Ye What Great Thing I Know   28
HENDON 7.7.7.7.7.7

Johan C. Schwedler, 1741 (1 Cor. 2:2; Gal. 6:14)
trans. by Benjamin H. Kennedy, 1863

H.A. César Malan, 1827
harm. by Lowell Mason, 1841

1. Ask ye what great thing I know, That delights and stirs me so? What the high reward I win? Whose the name I glory in? Jesus Christ, the crucified.
2. Who defeats my fiercest foes? Who consoles my saddest woes? Who revives my fainting heart, Healing all its hidden smart? Jesus Christ, the crucified.
3. Who is life in life to me? Who the death of death will be? Who will place me on His right, With the countless hosts of light? Jesus Christ, the crucified.
4. This is that great thing I know; This delights and stirs me so: Faith in Him Who died to save, Him Who triumphed o'er the grave: Jesus Christ, the crucified.

JESUS CHRIST

29 There Is a Green Hill Far Away
MEDITATION C.M.

Cecil Frances Alexander, 1848 — John H. Gower, 1890

1. There is a green hill far away, Outside a city wall, Where the dear Lord was crucified, Who died to save us all.
2. We may not know, we cannot tell What pains He had to bear; But we believe it was for us He hung and suffered there.
3. He died that we might be forgiven, He died to make us good, That we might go at last to heaven, Saved by His precious blood.
4. There was no other good enough To pay the price of sin; He only could unlock the gate Of heaven, and let us in.
5. Oh, dearly, dearly has He loved, And we must love Him, too, And trust in His redeeming blood, And try His works to do. A-men.

JESUS CHRIST

Immortal Love, Forever Full

SERENITY C.M.

John Greenleaf Whittier, 1866

arr. from William V. Wallace, 1856

30

1. Immortal Love, forever full, Forever flowing free, Forever shared, forever whole, A never-ebbing sea!
2. We may not climb the heavenly steeps To bring the Lord Christ down; In vain we search the lowest deeps, For Him no depths can drown.
3. But warm, sweet, tender, even yet A present help is He; And faith has still its Olivet, And love its Galilee.
4. The healing of His seamless dress Is by our beds of pain; We touch Him in life's throng and press, And we are whole again.
5. O Lord and Master of us all, What e'er our name or sign, We own Thy sway, we hear Thy call, We test our lives by Thine. A-men.

Words: Used by permission of Houghton Mifflin Company, authorized publishers.

JESUS CHRIST

31 I Love to Tell the Story
HANKEY 7.6.7.6.D with Refrain

Katherine Hankey, ca. 1868 William G. Fischer, 1869

1. I love to tell the sto - ry of un - seen things a -
2. I love to tell the sto - ry; more won - der - ful it
3. I love to tell the sto - ry; 'tis pleas - ant to re -
4. I love to tell the sto - ry, for those who know it

bove, Of Je - sus and His glo - ry, of Je - sus and His
seems Than all the gold - en fan - cies of all our gold - en
peat What seems, each time I tell it, more won - der - ful - ly
best Seem hun - ger - ing and thirst - ing to hear it like the

love. I love to tell the sto - ry be - cause I know 'tis
dreams. I love to tell the sto - ry; it did so much for
sweet. I love to tell the sto - ry, for some have nev - er
rest. And when, in scenes of glo - ry, I sing the new, new

JESUS CHRIST

true; It satisfies my longings as nothing else can do.
me; And that is just the reason I tell it now to thee.
heard The message of salvation from God's own holy Word.
song, 'Twill be the old, old story that I have loved so long.

Refrain

I love to tell the story; 'Twill be my theme in glory
To tell the old, old story of Jesus and His love.

JESUS CHRIST

32 Amen, Amen
Irregular

African-American spiritual

African-American spiritual
arr. Nelsie T. Johnson, 1988

1. See the lit-tle ba-by ___ Ly - ing in a man-ger ___ On Christ - mas ___ morn - ing. ___
2. See Him in the tem - ple ___ Talk - ing to the el - ders; ___ How they ___ all ___ mar - veled!
3. See Him at the sea - shore Preach-ing to the peo - ple, ___ Heal - ing all the sick ___ ones!
4. See Him in the gar - den ___ Pray - ing to the Fa - ther ___ In deep - est ___ sor - row!
5. See Him on the cross ___ Bear - ing all my sins ___ In bit - ter ___ ag - o - ny! ___
6. Yes, He died to save us ___ And He rose on Eas - ter; ___ Now He lives for-ev - er! ___
7. Al - le - lu - ia! ___ Je - sus is my Sav - ior, ___ And He lives for-ev - er! ___

A - men, A - men, A - men, A - men, A - men! A - men. A - men. A - men, A - men, A - men!

JESUS CHRIST

Oh, How I Love Jesus
33

OH, HOW I LOVE JESUS   C.M. with Refrain

Frederick Whitfield, 1855 — 19th century U.S.A. melody

1. There is a Name I love to hear, I love to sing Its worth;
   It sounds like music in my ear, The sweetest Name on earth.
2. It tells me of a Savior's love, Who died to set me free;
   It tells me of His precious blood, The sinner's perfect plea.
3. It tells of One Whose loving heart Can feel my deepest woe;
   Who in each sorrow bears a part That none can bear below.

Refrain
Oh, how I love Jesus, Oh, how I love Jesus, Oh, how I love Jesus, Because He first loved me!

JESUS CHRIST

34   I Have Found a Friend in Jesus
The Lily of the Valley
SALVATIONIST   Irregular with Refrain

Charles W. Fry (1837–1882)

William S. Hays (1837–1907)
adapt. by Charles W. Fry

1. I have found a friend in Jesus, He's everything to me,
   He's the fairest of ten thousand to my soul;
   The Lily of the Valley, in Him alone I see
   All I need to cleanse and make me fully whole.

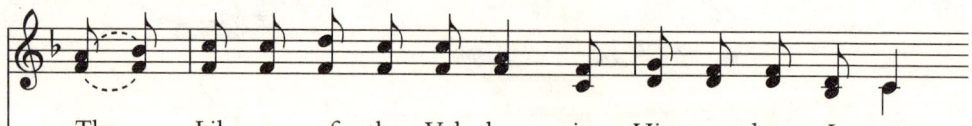

2. He all my grief has taken, and all my sorrows borne;
   In temptation He's my strong and mighty tower;
   I have all for Him forsaken, and all my idols torn
   From my heart and now He keeps me by His power.

3. He will never, never leave me, nor yet forsake me here,
   While I live by faith and do His blessed will;
   A wall of fire about me, I've nothing now to fear,
   With His manna He my hungry soul shall fill.

JESUS CHRIST

In sor-row He's my com-fort, in troub-le He's my stay;
Though all the world for-sake me, and Sa-tan tempt me sore,
Then sweep-ing up to glo-ry to see His bless-ed face,

He tells me ev-ery care on Him to roll:
Through Je-sus I shall safe-ly reach the goal:
Where riv-ers of de-light shall ev-er roll:

Refrain
He's the Lil-y of the Val-ley, the Bright and Morn-ing Star,

He's the fair-est of ten thous-and to my soul.

JESUS CHRIST

35   Jesus, Keep Me near the Cross
NEAR THE CROSS   7.6.7.6 with Refrain

Fanny J. Crosby, 1869   William H. Doane, 1869

1. Je-sus, keep me near the cross; There a pre-cious foun-tain,
2. Near the cross, a trem-bling soul, Love and mer-cy found me;
3. Near the cross! O Lamb of God, Bring its scenes be-fore me;
4. Near the cross I'll watch and wait, Hop-ing, trust-ing ev-er,

Free to all, a heal-ing stream, Flows from Cal-vary's moun-tain.
There the bright and Morn-ing Star Sheds Its beams a-round me.
Help me walk from day to day With its shad-ow o'er me.
Till I reach the gold-en strand Just be-yond the riv-er.

Refrain

In the cross, in the cross Be my glo-ry ev-er,

Till my rap-tured soul shall find Rest be-yond the riv-er.

JESUS CHRIST

In the Garden
I Come to the Garden Alone
GARDEN   8.9.5.5.7 with Refrain

36

C. Austin Miles, 1913 (Jn. 20:11–18)

C. Austin Miles, 1913
adapt. by Charles H. Webb, 1987

1. I come to the garden alone While the dew is still on the roses, And the voice I hear falling on my ear The Son of God disclose.
2. He speaks, and the sound of His voice Is so sweet, the birds hush their singing, And the melody that He gave to me Within my heart is ringing.
3. I'd stay in the garden with Him Though the night around me be falling, But He bids me go; through the voice of woe His voice to me is calling.

Refrain
And He walks with me, and He talks with me, And He tells me I am His own; And the joy we share as we tarry there None other has ever known.

JESUS CHRIST

37 He Lives

ACKLEY 76.76.76.74 with Refrain

Alfred H. Ackley, 1933 — Alfred H. Ackley, 1933

1. I serve a ris-en Sav-ior, He's in the world to-day;
2. In all the world a-round me I see His lov-ing care,
3. Re-joice, re-joice, O Chris-tian, lift up your voice and sing

I know that He is liv-ing, what-ev-er foes may say.
And though my heart grows wear-y, I nev-er will de-spair.
E-ter-nal hal-le-lu-jahs to Je-sus Christ the King!

I see His hand of mer-cy, I hear His voice of cheer,
I know that He is lead-ing through all the storm-y blast;
The hope of all who seek Him, the help of all who find;

And just the time I need Him, He's al-ways near.
The day of His ap-pear-ing will come at last.
None oth-er is so lov-ing, so good and kind.

Words and Music: © 1933; renewed 1962 Word Music, Inc. (ASCAP), 65 Music Square West, Nashville, TN 37203. All rights reserved. Made in the U.S.A. International copyright secured. Used by permission.

JESUS CHRIST

Refrain

He lives, He lives, Christ Jesus lives to-day!
(He lives,) *(He lives,)*

He walks with me and talks with me along life's narrow way.

He lives, He lives, salvation to impart!
(He lives,) *(He lives,)*

You ask me how I know He lives? He lives within my heart.

JESUS CHRIST

38 Up from the Grave He Arose

CHRIST AROSE   6.5.6.4 with Refrain

Robert Lowry, 1874   Robert Lowry, 1874

1. Low in the grave He lay,
2. Vain-ly they watch His bed, Jesus, my Savior;
3. Death can-not keep its prey,

Wait-ing the com-ing day,
Vain-ly they seal the dead, Jesus, my Lord!
He tore the bars a-way,

Refrain

Up from the grave He a-rose,
(He a-rose,)
With a might-y tri-umph o'er His foes;
(o'er His foes,)
He a-

JESUS CHRIST

JESUS CHRIST

39 I Danced in the Morning
SIMPLE GIFTS   Irregular with Refrain

Sydney Carter, 1963

American Shaker melody
harm. Sydney Carter, 1963

1. I danced in the morning when the world was begun, And I danced in the moon and the stars and the sun, And I came down from heaven, and I
2. I danced for the scribe and the Pharisee, But they would not dance, and they would not follow Me; I danced for the fishermen, for
3. I danced on the Sabbath and I cured the lame; The holy people said it was a shame. They whipped, and they stripped, and they
4. I danced on a Friday when the sky turned black; It's hard to dance with the devil on your back. They buried My body, and they
5. They cut Me down, and I leap up high; I am the life that will never, never die; I'll live in you if you'll

Words and Music: © 1963 by Stainer & Bell Ltd. (admin. by Hope Publishing Co., Carol Stream, IL 60188). All rights reserved. Used by permission.

JESUS CHRIST

danced on the earth; At Beth-le-hem I ___ had My birth.
James and John; They came with Me and the dance went on.
hung Me high And left Me ___ there on a cross to die.
thought I'd ___ gone: But I am the dance, and I still go on.
live in ___ Me; I am the Lord of the Dance, said He.

Refrain

Dance, then, wher-ev-er you may be; I am the Lord of the
Dance, said He, And I'll lead you all, wher-ev-er you may be,
And I'll lead you all in the dance, said He.

40 Fairest Lord Jesus

CRUSADERS' HYMN 5.6.8.5.5.8

Münster *Gesangbuch*, 1677
trans. *Church Chorals and Choir Studies*, 1850, alt.

Silesian folk melody
in *Schlesische Volkslieder*, 1842

1. Fairest Lord Jesus, Ruler of all nature,
O Thou of God to earth come down,
Thee will I cherish, Thee will I honor,
Thou, my soul's glory, joy, and crown.

2. Fair are the meadows, Fairer still the woodlands,
Robed in the blooming garb of spring;
Jesus is fairer, Jesus is purer,
Who makes the woeful heart to sing.

3. Fair is the sunshine, Fairer still the moonlight,
And all the twinkling, starry host:
Jesus shines brighter, Jesus shines purer
Than all the angels heaven can boast.

JESUS CHRIST

Tell Me the Stories of Jesus

41

STORIES OF JESUS 8.4.8.4.5.4.5.4

William H. Parker, 1885
Frederic A. Challinor, 1905

Unison or duet

1. Tell me the sto-ries of Je - sus I love to hear;
2. First let me hear how the chil - dren stood 'round His knee,
3. In - to the cit - y I'd fol - low the chil - dren's band,

Things I would ask Him to tell me if He were here:
And I shall fan - cy His bless - ing rest - ing on me;
Wav - ing a branch of the palm tree high in my hand;

Scenes by the way - side, tales of the sea,
Words full of kind - ness, deeds full of grace,
One of His her - alds, yes, I would sing

Sto - ries of Je - sus, tell them to me.
All in the love - light of Je - sus' face.
Loud - est ho - san - nas, "Je - sus is King!" A - men.

Words and Music: copyright by The National Sunday School Union. Used by permission.

JESUS CHRIST

42 Praise Him! Praise Him!
JOYFUL SONG   12.10.12.10.11.10.11.10

Fanny J. Crosby, 1869 — Chester G. Allen, 1869

1.–3. Praise Him! Praise Him! Jesus, our blessed Redeemer!

1. Sing, O earth, His wonderful love proclaim!
2. For our sins He suffered and bled and died;
3. Heavenly portals loud with hosannas ring!

Hail Him! Hail Him! Highest archangels in glory;
He our Rock, our hope of eternal salvation,
Jesus, Savior, reigneth forever and ever;

Strength and honor give to His holy Name!
Hail Him! Hail Him! Jesus the Crucified.
Crown Him! Crown Him! Prophet and Priest and King!

JESUS CHRIST

Like a shep - herd Je - sus will guard His chil - dren;
Sound His prais - es! Je - sus Who bore our sor - rows;
Christ is com - ing! O - ver the world vic - to - rious,

In His arms He car - ries them all day long:
Love un - bound - ed, won - der - ful, deep, and strong:
Power and glo - ry un - to the Lord be - long:

Refrain
Praise Him! Praise Him! tell of His ex - cel - lent great - ness;

Praise Him! Praise Him ev - er in joy - ful song!

JESUS CHRIST

43 Of the Father's Love Begotten
DIVINUM MYSTERIUM   8.7.8.7.8.7.7

Aurelius Clemens Prudentius (348–413)
trans. John Mason Neale, 1854,
and Henry Williams Baker, 1859

Plainsong, Mode V
harm. C. Winfred Douglas, 1940

1. Of the Father's love be-got-ten, Ere the worlds be-gan to be,
2. O ye heights of heaven a-dore Him; An-gel hosts, His prais-es sing;
3. Christ, to Thee with God the Fa-ther, And, O Ho-ly Ghost, to Thee,

He is Al-pha and O-meg-a, He the source, the end-ing He,
Powers, do-min-ions, bow be-fore Him, And ex-tol our God and King;
Hymn and chant and high thanks-giv-ing And un-wear-ied prais-es be:

Of the things that are, that have been, And that fu-ture years shall see,
Let no tongue on earth be si-lent, Ev-ery voice in con-cert ring,
Hon-or, glo-ry, and do-min-ion, And e-ter-nal vic-to-ry,

Music: © 1943, 1961, 1985 Church Pension Fund. Used by permission.

Ev-er-more and ev-er-more! A - men.

Jesus, the Very Thought of Thee   44
ST. AGNES   C.M.

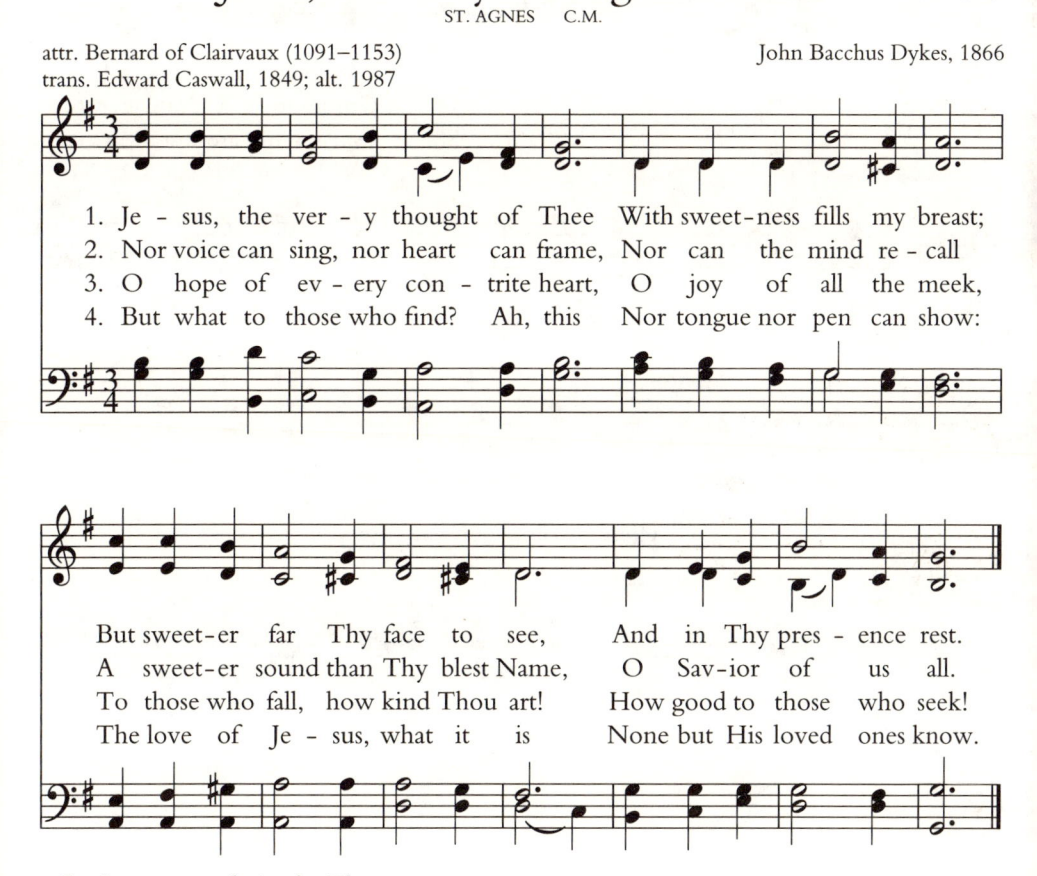

attr. Bernard of Clairvaux (1091–1153)
trans. Edward Caswall, 1849; alt. 1987
John Bacchus Dykes, 1866

1. Je-sus, the ver-y thought of Thee With sweet-ness fills my breast;
2. Nor voice can sing, nor heart can frame, Nor can the mind re-call
3. O hope of ev-ery con-trite heart, O joy of all the meek,
4. But what to those who find? Ah, this Nor tongue nor pen can show:

But sweet-er far Thy face to see, And in Thy pres-ence rest.
A sweet-er sound than Thy blest Name, O Sav-ior of us all.
To those who fall, how kind Thou art! How good to those who seek!
The love of Je-sus, what it is None but His loved ones know.

5. Jesus, our only joy be Thou,
   As Thou our prize wilt be;
   Jesus, be Thou our glory now,
   And through eternity.

JESUS CHRIST

45 There Is Power in the Blood
POWER IN THE BLOOD   Irregular

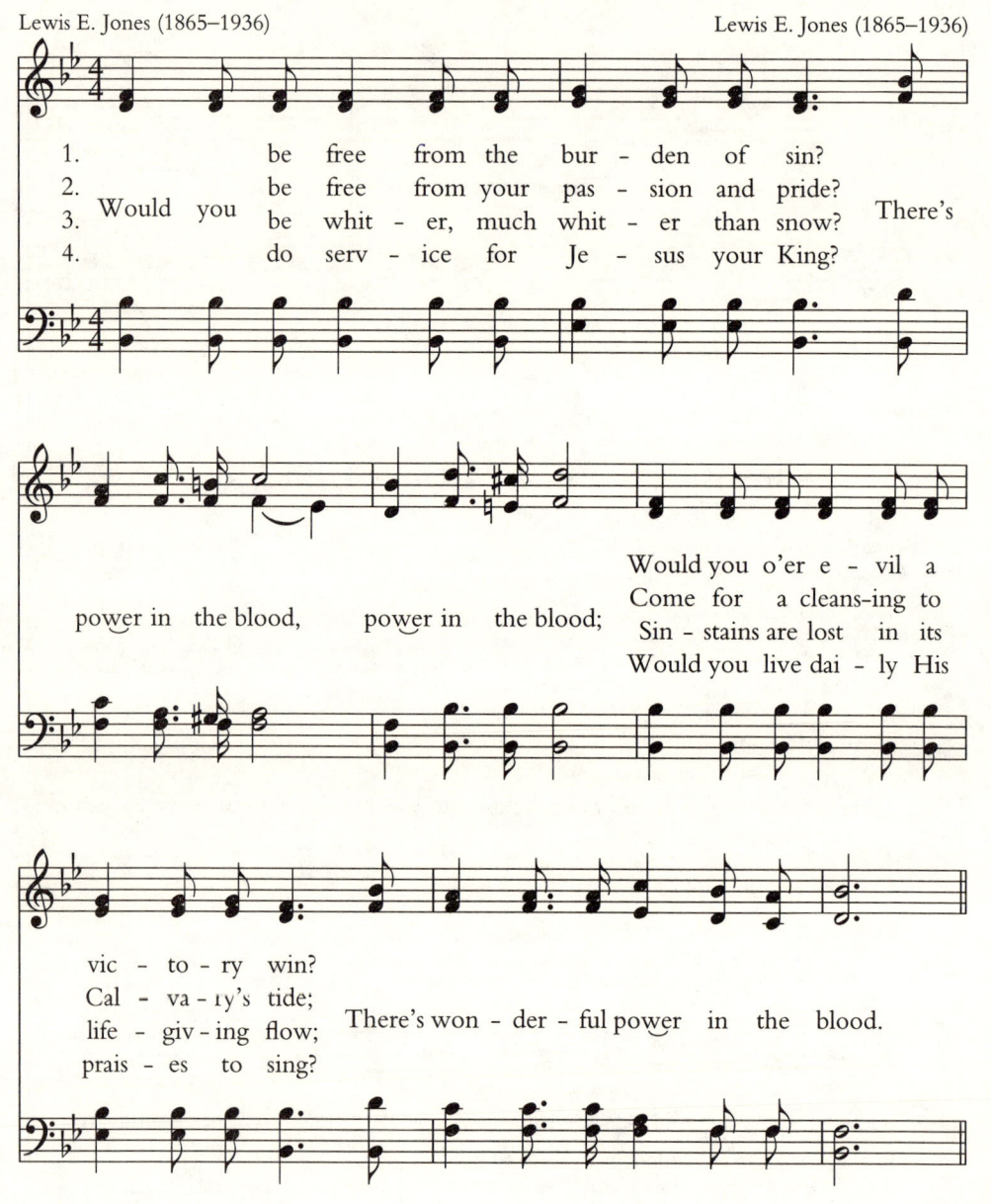

Lewis E. Jones (1865–1936)   Lewis E. Jones (1865–1936)

1. Would you be free from the burden of sin?
2. Would you be free from your passion and pride?
3. Would you be whiter, much whiter than snow?
4. Would you do service for Jesus your King?

There's power in the blood, power in the blood;

Would you o'er evil a victory win?
Come for a cleansing to Calvary's tide;
Sin-stains are lost in its life-giving flow;
Would you live daily His praises to sing?

There's wonderful power in the blood.

JESUS CHRIST

Refrain

There is power, power, won-der-work-ing power in the
(there is)
blood of the Lamb; There is power, power,
(in the blood) *(of the Lamb;)* *(there is)*
won-der-work-ing power in the pre-cious blood of the Lamb.

HOLY SPIRIT

46 Every Time I Feel the Spirit
PENTECOST   Irregular

African-American spiritual

African-American spiritual
arr. Joseph T. Jones (1902–1983)
adapt. Melva W. Costen, 1989

Refrain

Ev-ery time I feel the Spir-it mov-ing in my heart I will pray.

Yes, ev-ery time I feel the Spir-it mov-ing in my heart I will pray.

1. Up-on the moun-tain, when my Lord spoke, Out of God's mouth came ___ fire and smoke. Looked all a-round me, it
2. Jor-dan riv-er, chil-ly and cold, It chills the bod-y but not the soul. There is but one train up-

Music: adaptation © 1990 Melva W. Costen. All rights reserved. Used by permission.

HOLY SPIRIT

D.C.

looked so fine, Till I asked my Lord if all was mine.
on this track; It runs to heav-en and then right back.

Breathe on Me, Breath of God   47
TRENTHAM   S.M.

Edwin Hatch, 1886   Robert Jackson, 1894

1. Breathe on me, Breath of God, Fill me with life a-new,
2. Breathe on me, Breath of God, Un-til my heart is pure,
3. Breathe on me, Breath of God, Till I am whol-ly Thine,
4. Breathe on me, Breath of God, So shall I nev-er die,

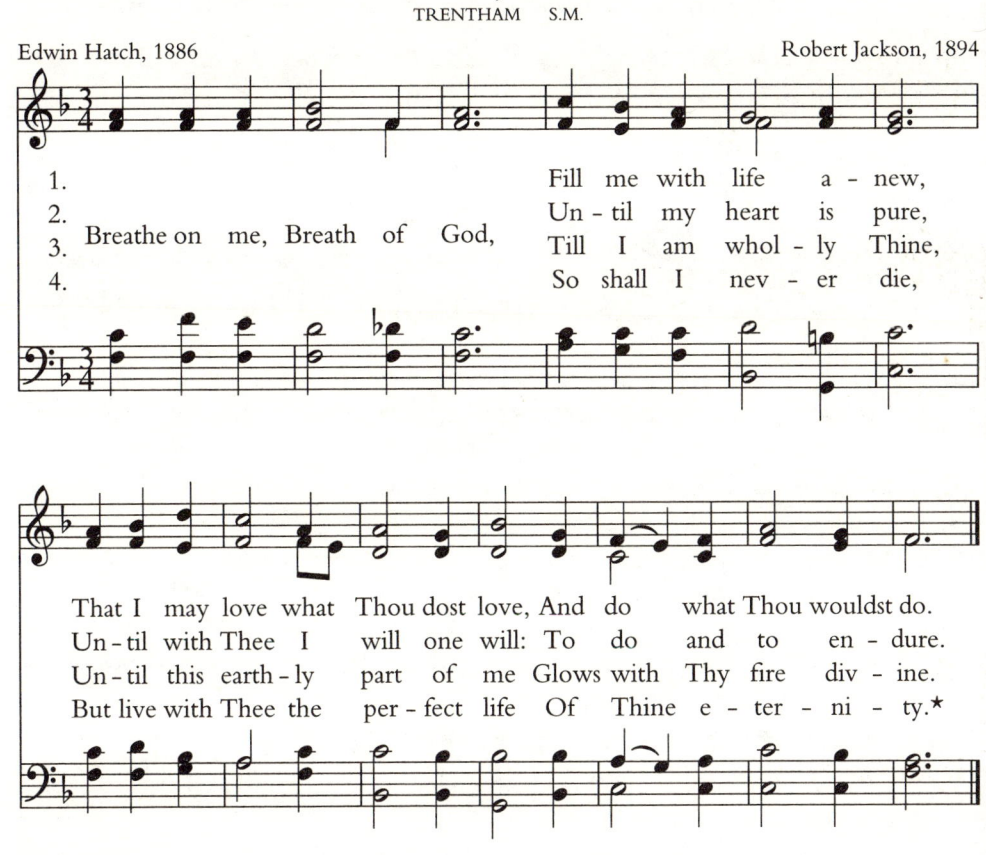

That I may love what Thou dost love, And do what Thou wouldst do.
Un-til with Thee I will one will: To do and to en-dure.
Un-til this earth-ly part of me Glows with Thy fire div-ine.
But live with Thee the per-fect life Of Thine e-ter-ni-ty.*

*Repeat stanza 1.

HOLY SPIRIT

48. Open My Eyes, That I May See

OPEN MY EYES 8.8.9.8 with Refrain

Clara H. Scott, 1895

Clara H. Scott, 1895

1. eyes, that I may see Glimpses of truth Thou hast for me;
2. O-pen my ears, that I may hear Voices of truth Thou sendest clear;
3. mouth, and let me bear Gladly the warm truth everywhere;

Place in my hands the wonderful key That shall un-clasp and set me free.
And while the wave-notes fall on my ear, Ev-ery-thing false will dis-ap-pear.
O-pen my heart, and let me pre-pare Love with Thy chil-dren thus to share.

Refrain

Si-lent-ly now I wait for Thee, Read-y, my God, Thy will to see;

O-pen my ears, il-lu-mine me, Spir-it div-ine!
eyes,
heart,

HOLY SPIRIT

Spirit of God, Descend upon My Heart

49

MORECAMBE 10.10.10.10

George Croly, 1854   Frederick Cook Atkinson, 1870

1. Spirit of God, descend upon my heart;
   Wean it from earth, through all its pulses move;
   Stoop to my weakness, mighty as Thou art,
   And make me love Thee as I ought to love.

2. Hast Thou not bid us love Thee, God and King;
   All, all Thine own: soul, heart, and strength, and mind?
   I see Thy cross, there teach my heart to cling.
   Oh, let me seek Thee, and oh, let me find!

3. Teach me to feel that Thou art always nigh;
   Teach me the struggles of the soul to bear,
   To check the rising doubt, the rebel sigh;
   Teach me the patience of unanswered prayer.

4. Teach me to love Thee as Thine angels love,
   One holy passion filling all my frame;
   The baptism of the heaven-descended Dove,
   My heart an altar, and Thy love the flame.

HOLY SCRIPTURE

50 O Word of God Incarnate
MUNICH 7.6.7.6.D

William Walsham How, 1867
as in *Psalter Hymnal*, 1987

Neuvermehrtes Meiningisches Gesangbuch, 1693
adapt. Felix Mendelssohn, 1847

1. O Word of God incarnate, O Wisdom from on high,
   O Truth unchanged, unchanging, O Light of our dark sky:
   We praise You for the radiance That from the hallowed page,
   A lantern to our footsteps, Shines on from age to age.

2. The church from You, dear Savior, Received this gift divine,
   And still that light is lifted On all the earth to shine.
   It is the chart and compass That, all life's voyage through,
   Amid the rocks and quick-sands, Still guides, O Christ, to You.

3. Oh, make Your church, dear Savior, A lamp of purest gold
   To bear before the nations Your true light, as of old:
   Oh, teach Your wandering pilgrims By this our path to trace,
   Till, clouds and storms thus ended, We see You face to face.

HOLY SCRIPTURE

Break Thou the Bread of Life   51
BREAD OF LIFE 6.4.6.4.D

Mary Artemesia Lathbury, 1877, alt. William Fiske Sherwin, 1877, alt.

1. Break Thou the bread of life, dear Lord, to me,
As Thou didst break the loaves beside the sea;
Beyond the sacred page I seek Thee, Lord;
My spirit pants for Thee, O living Word!

2. Bless Thou the truth, dear Lord, now unto me,
As Thou didst bless the bread by Galilee;
Then shall all bondage cease, all fetters fall;
And I shall find my peace, my all in all.

HOLY SCRIPTURE

52. Wonderful Words of Life
WORDS OF LIFE 8.6.8.6.6.6

Philip P. Bliss, 1874 *Philip P. Bliss, 1874*

1. Sing them o-ver a-gain to me, Won-der-ful words of life;
2. Christ, the bless-ed One, gives to all Won-der-ful words of life;
3. Sweet-ly ech-o the gos-pel call, Won-der-ful words of life;

Let me more of their beau-ty see,
Sin-ner, list to the lov-ing call,
Off-er par-don and peace to all,

Words of life and beau-ty Teach me faith and du-ty.
All so free-ly giv-en, Woo-ing us to heav-en.
Je-sus, on-ly Sav-ior, Sanc-ti-fy for-ev-er.

Refrain

Beau-ti-ful words, won-der-ful words, Won-der-ful words of life;

Beau-ti-ful words, won-der-ful words, Won-der-ful words of life.

LIFE IN CHRIST

Master, No Offering Costly and Sweet 53
LOVE'S OFFERING 6.4.6.4.6.6.6.4.

Edwin P. Parker, 1888 — Edwin P. Parker, 1888

1. Master, no offering Costly and sweet,
May we, like Magdalene, Lay at Thy feet;
Yet may love's incense rise, Sweeter than sacrifice,
Dear Lord, to Thee, Dear Lord, to Thee. A-men.

2. Daily our lives would show Weakness made strong,
Toilsome and gloomy ways Brightened with song;
Some deeds of kindness done, Some souls by patience won,
Dear Lord, to Thee, Dear Lord, to Thee.

3. Some word of hope for hearts Burdened with fears,
Some balm of peace for eyes Blinded with tears,
Some dews of mercy shed, Some wayward footsteps led,
Dear Lord, to Thee, Dear Lord, to Thee.

4. Thus, in Thy service, Lord, Till eventide
Closes the day of life, May we abide;
And when earth's labors cease, Bid us depart in peace,
Dear Lord, to Thee, Dear Lord, to Thee.

LIFE IN CHRIST

54 Jesus Is Tenderly Calling Thee Home
JESUS IS CALLING   10.8.10.7 with Refrain

Fanny Crosby (1820–1915)

George C. Stebbins (1846–1945)
harm. 1954

1. Jesus is tenderly calling thee home— Calling today,
   calling today; Why from the sunshine of love wilt thou roam
   Farther and farther away?
2. Jesus is calling the weary to rest— Calling today,
   calling today; Bring Him thy burden and thou shalt be blest:
   He will not turn thee away.
3. Jesus is waiting— oh, come to Him now— Waiting today,
   waiting today; Come with thy sins; at His feet lowly bow;
   Come, and no longer delay.
4. Jesus is pleading; oh, list to His voice: Hear Him today,
   hear Him today; They who believe on His name shall rejoice;
   Quickly arise and away.

Refrain

Calling today,
(Calling, calling today, today,)

Music: copyright 1955 by John Ribble.

LIFE IN CHRIST

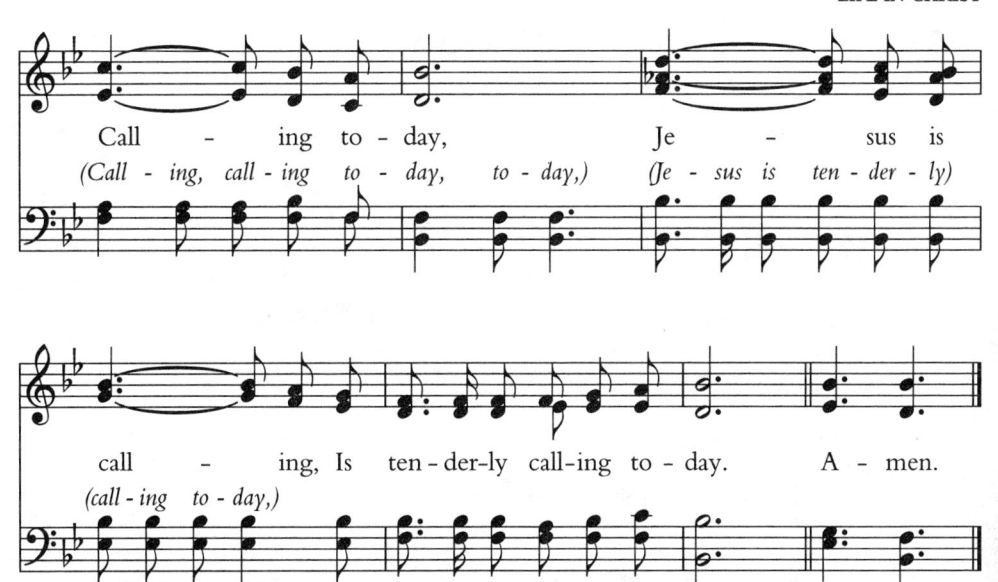

LIFE IN CHRIST

55 Be Thou My Vision
SLANE   10.10.9.10

ancient Irish poem
trans. Mary E. Byrne, 1905
vers. Eleanor Hull, 1912; alt.

Irish ballad
harm. David Evans, 1927

1. Be Thou my vis-ion, O Lord of my heart;
2. Rich-es I heed not, nor vain, emp-ty praise,
3. Be Thou my wis-dom, and Thou my true word;

Nought be all else to me, save that Thou art—
Thou mine in-her-it-ance, now and al-ways:
I ev-er with Thee and Thou with me, Lord;

Music: harmonization from the *Revised Church Hymnary 1927*. Used by permission of Oxford University Press.

LIFE IN CHRIST

Thou my best thought, by day or by night,
Thou and Thou on - ly, first in my heart,
Heart of my own heart, what - ev - er be - fall,

Wak - ing or sleep - ing, Thy pres - ence my light.
Great God of heav - en, my treas - ure Thou art.
Still be my vis - ion, O Rul - er of all.

LIFE IN CHRIST

56 Lead, Kindly Light
LUX BENIGNA   10.4.10.4.10.10

John Henry Newman, 1833   John B. Dykes, 1865

1. Lead, kind-ly Light, a-mid th' en-cir-cling gloom, Lead Thou me on; The night is dark, and I am far from home; Lead Thou me on: Keep Thou my feet; I do not ask to see The dis-tant scene—one step e-nough for me.
2. I was not ev-er thus, nor prayed that Thou Shouldst lead me on; I loved to choose and see my path; but now Lead Thou me on. I loved the gar-ish day, and, spite of fears, Pride ruled my will: re-mem-ber not past years.
3. So long Thy power hath blest me, sure it still Will lead me on, O'er moor and fen, o'er crag and tor-rent, till The night is gone; And with the morn those an-gel fa-ces smile, Which I have loved long since, and lost a-while. A-men.

Note: Alternate tune: SANDON.

LIFE IN CHRIST

Dear Lord and Father of Mankind   57
REST   8.6.8.8.6

John Greenleaf Whittier, 1872 — Frederick Charles Maker, 1887

1. *Dear Lord and Father of mankind, Forgive our foolish ways; Re-clothe us in our rightful mind, In purer lives Thy service find, In deeper reverence, praise.
2. In simple trust like theirs who heard, Beside the Syrian sea, The gracious calling of the Lord, Let us, like them, without a word Rise up and follow Thee.
3. O Sabbath rest by Galilee, O calm of hills above, Where Jesus knelt to share with Thee The silence of eternity, Interpreted by love!
4. Drop Thy still dews of quietness, Till all our strivings cease; Take from our souls the strain and stress, And let our ordered lives confess The beauty of Thy peace.

5. Breathe through the heats of our desire
   Thy coolness and Thy balm;
   Let sense be dumb, let flesh retire;
   Speak through the earthquake, wind, and fire,
   O still, small voice of calm!

Note: Alternate tune: REPTON, *The Presbyterian Hymnal* # 419

Note: Or "Dear Lord, Creator good and kind."

LIFE IN CHRIST

58 Whak Shil Hahn Nah Eh Kahn Jeung
Blessed Assurance, Jesus Is Mine!

ASSURANCE 9.10.9.9 with Refrain

Fanny Jane Crosby, 1873
transliteration of Korean: Myung Ja Yue, 1989

Phoebe Palmer Knapp, 1873

1. Ye su rul nae ga joo ro mee duh Sung nyung gwa
2. Ye su keh maat kin nah eh ma um Sa rahng eh

1. Bless-ed as-sur-ance, Je-sus is mine! O what a
2. Per-fect sub-mis-sion, per-fect de-light, Vi-sions of

pee ro ssuh kuh dum nah nee Seh sahng eh in nun
sok sah gim tu ru myun suh Heen oh sul ee bun

fore-taste of glo-ry di-vine! Heir of sal-va-tion,
rap-ture now burst on my sight; An-gels, de-scend-ing,

nae young hon ee Ha nu reh young gwang noo ree doh dah
chun sah dul gwa Shin bee hahn whan sahng bo ree ro dah

pur-chase of God, Born of His Spir-it, washed in His blood.
bring from a-bove Ech-oes of mer-cy, whis-pers of love.

Text: transliteration © 1990 Westminster/John Knox Press. All rights reserved.

LIFE IN CHRIST

Hooryum
Refrain

Ee go she nah eh kahn jeung ee yo Ee go she nah eh chan song ee rah Nah sah nun dong ahn ggeun im up see Ye su eh ee rum chan song hah ree

This is my sto-ry, this is my song, Prais-ing my Sav-ior all the day long; This is my sto-ry, this is my song, Prais-ing my Sav-ior all the day long.

3. Joo ahn eh ees suh jeul guh wuh rah
   Ma um eh Poong nahng ee jahm jah doh dah
   Seh sahng doh up go nah doh up go
   Sa rahng eh joo mahn bo ee doh dah
   Hooryum

3. Perfect submission, all is at rest,
   I in my Savior am happy and blest,
   Watching and waiting, looking above,
   Filled with His goodness, lost in His love.
   Refrain

LIFE IN CHRIST

59 Who Is on the Lord's Side?
ARMAGEDDON 6.5.6.5.6.5.D

Frances Ridley Havergal, 1877

German melody
adapted by John Goss, 1871

1. Who is on the Lord's side? Who will serve the King?
   Who will be His helpers, Other lives to bring?
   Who will leave the world's side? Who will face the foe?
2. Not for weight of glory, Not for crown and palm,
   Enter we the army, Raise the warrior psalm;
   But for Love that claimeth Lives for whom He died:
3. Fierce may be the conflict, Strong may be the foe,
   But the King's own army None can overthrow:
   'Round His standard ranging, Victory is secure;

LIFE IN CHRIST

Who is on the Lord's side? Who for Him will go?
He whom Jesus nameth Must be on His side.
For His truth unchanging Makes the triumph sure.

By Thy call of mercy,
By Thy love constraining, By Thy grace divine,
Joyfully enlisting

Last time

We are on the Lord's side, Saviour, we are Thine. A-men.

LIFE IN CHRIST

60 Once to Every Man and Nation

EBENEZER (TON-Y-BOTEL) 8.7.8.7.D

James Russell Lowell, 1845, alt. Thomas John Williams, 1890

1. Once to ev-ery man and na-tion Comes the moment to de-cide, In the strife of truth with false-hood, For the good or
2. Then to side with truth is no-ble, When we share her wretch-ed crust, Ere her cause bring fame and prof-it, And 'tis pros-perous
3. Though the cause of e-vil pros-per, Yet 'tis truth a-lone is strong; Though her por-tion be the scaf-fold, And up-on the

Music: copyright by Gwenlyn Evans, Ltd. Used by permission.

LIFE IN CHRIST

e - vil side; Some great cause, some new de -
to be just; Then it is the brave man
throne be wrong, Yet that scaf - fold sways the

cis - ion, Off - ering each the bloom or blight,
choos - es While the cow - ard stands a - side,
fu - ture, And, be - hind the dim un - known,

And the choice goes by for - ev - er
Till the mul - ti - tude make vir - tue
Stand - eth God with - in the shad - ow

'Twixt that dark - ness and that light.
Of the faith they had de - nied.
Keep - ing watch a - bove His own. A - men.

LIFE IN CHRIST

61   O Jesus, I Have Promised
NYLAND   7.6.7.6.D

John Ernest Bode, 1866

Finnish folk melody
adapt. and harm. David Evans, 1927

1. O Jesus, I have promised To serve Thee to the end;
2. Oh, let me feel Thee near me! The world is ev-er near;
3. Oh, let me hear Thee speaking In accents clear and still,
4. O Jesus, Thou hast promised To all who follow Thee

Be Thou forever near me, My Master and my friend;
I see the sights that dazzle, The tempting sounds I hear;
Above the storms of passion, The murmurs of self-will;
That where Thou art in glory There shall Thy servant be;

♩ = 46–50

Note: Alternate tune: ANGEL'S STORY, *The Presbyterian Hymnal* # 388

Music: adaptation and harmonization from the *Revised Church Hymnary*, 1927; used by permission of Oxford University Press.

LIFE IN CHRIST

I shall not fear the battle If Thou art by my side,
Nor wander from the pathway If Thou wilt be my guide.

My foes are ev-er near me, A-round me and with-in;
But, Jesus, draw Thou near-er And shield my soul from sin.

O speak to re-as-sure me, To has-ten or con-trol;
O speak, and make me lis-ten, Thou guard-ian of my soul.

And, Je-sus, I have prom-ised To serve Thee to the end;
O give me grace to fol-low, My Mas-ter and my friend.

LIFE IN CHRIST

62 I Know the Lord's Laid His Hands on Me
HANDS ON ME   Irregular

Traditional
Spiritual

Refrain

Oh, I know the Lord, I know the Lord, I know the Lord's laid His hands on me, O I know the Lord, I know the Lord, I know the Lord's laid His hands on me.

Fine

1. Did ev-er you see the like be-fore?
2. Oh, was-n't that a hap-py day,
3. Some seek the Lord and don't seek Him right,
4. My Lord's done just what He said,

I know the

LIFE IN CHRIST

LIFE IN CHRIST

63 Guide My Feet
GUIDE MY FEET 8.8.8.10

African-American spiritual

African-American spiritual
harm. Wendell Whalum (1932–1987)

1. Guide my feet while I run this race, *(yes, my Lord!)* Guide my feet while I run this race, Guide my feet while I run this race, For I don't want to run this race in vain! *(race in vain!)*
2. Hold my hand while I run this race, *(yes, my Lord!)* Hold my hand while I run this race, Hold my hand while I run this race, For I don't want to run this race in vain! *(race in vain!)*
3. Stand by me while I run this race, *(yes, my Lord!)* Stand by me while I run this race, Stand by me while I run this race, For I don't want to run this race in vain! *(race in vain!)*
4. I'm Your child while I run this race, *(yes, my Lord!)* I'm Your child while I run this race, I'm Your child while I run this race, For I don't want to run this race in vain! *(race in vain!)*

5. Search my heart . . .

6. Guide my feet . . .

Music: harmonization © by the estate of Wendell Whalum. Used by permission.

LIFE IN CHRIST

Come, Thou Fount of Every Blessing

NETTLETON 8.7.8.7.D

Robert Robinson, c. 1758

Wyeth's *Repository of Sacred Music*, 1813

64

1. Come, Thou Fount of ev-ery bless-ing, Tune my heart to sing Thy grace;
Streams of mer-cy, nev-er ceas-ing, Call for songs of loud-est praise.
Teach me some mel-od-ious son-net, Sung by flam-ing tongues a-bove;
Praise the mount! I'm fixed up-on it, Mount of God's un-chang-ing love!

2. Here I raise my Eb-en-e-zer, Hith-er by Thy help I'm come;
And I hope, by Thy good pleas-ure, Safe-ly to ar-rive at home.
Je-sus sought me when a stran-ger, Wan-dering from the fold of God;
He, to res-cue me from dan-ger, In-ter-posed His pre-cious blood.

3. O to grace how great a debt-or Dai-ly I'm con-strained to be!
Let that grace now, like a fet-ter, Bind my wan-dering heart to Thee:
Prone to wan-der, Lord, I feel it, Prone to leave the God I love;
Here's my heart, O take and seal it, Seal it for Thy courts a-bove.

LIFE IN CHRIST

65 O Master, Let Me Walk with Thee
MARYTON L.M.

Washington Gladden, 1879 Henry Percy Smith, 1874

1. O Master, let me walk with Thee In lowly paths of service free; Tell me Thy secret; help me bear The strain of toil, the fret of care.
2. Help me the slow of heart to move By some clear, winning word of love; Teach me the wayward feet to stay, And guide them in the homeward way.
3. Teach me Thy patience; still with Thee In closer, dearer company, In work that keeps faith sweet and strong, In trust that triumphs over wrong.
4. In hope that sends a shining ray Far down the future's broadening way; In peace that only Thou canst give, With Thee, O Master, let me live.

More Love to Thee, O Christ

MORE LOVE TO THEE 6.4.6.4.6.6.4.4

Elizabeth Payson Prentiss, 1856

William Howard Doane, 1870

66

LIFE IN CHRIST

1. More love to Thee, O Christ, More love to Thee!
   Hear Thou the prayer I make On bended knee.
   This is my earnest plea:
   More love to Thee, More love to Thee!

2. Once earthly joy I craved, Sought peace and rest;
   Now Thee alone I seek, Give what is best.
   This all my prayer shall be: More love, O Christ, to Thee,
   More love to Thee, More love to Thee!

3. Then shall my latest breath Whisper Thy praise;
   This be the parting cry My heart shall raise.
   This still its prayer shall be:
   More love to Thee, More love to Thee!

LIFE IN CHRIST

67 How Firm a Foundation
FOUNDATION 11.11.11.11

"K" in *A Selection of Hymns,* 1787
ed. John Rippon; alt.

American folk melody
Funk's *Genuine Church Music,* 1832

1. How firm a foun-da-tion, ye saints of the Lord,
2. "Fear not, I am with thee, O be not dis-mayed,
3. "When through the deep wa-ters I call thee to go,
4. "When through fi-ery tri-als thy path-way shall lie,

Is laid for your faith in God's ex-cel-lent Word!
For I am thy God, and will still give thee aid;
The riv-ers of sor-row shall not o-ver-flow;
My grace, all-suf-fi-cient, shall be thy sup-ply;

What more can be said than to you God hath said,
I'll strength-en thee, help thee, and cause thee to stand,
For I will be near thee, thy troub-les to bless,
The flame shall not hurt thee; I on-ly de-sign

LIFE IN CHRIST

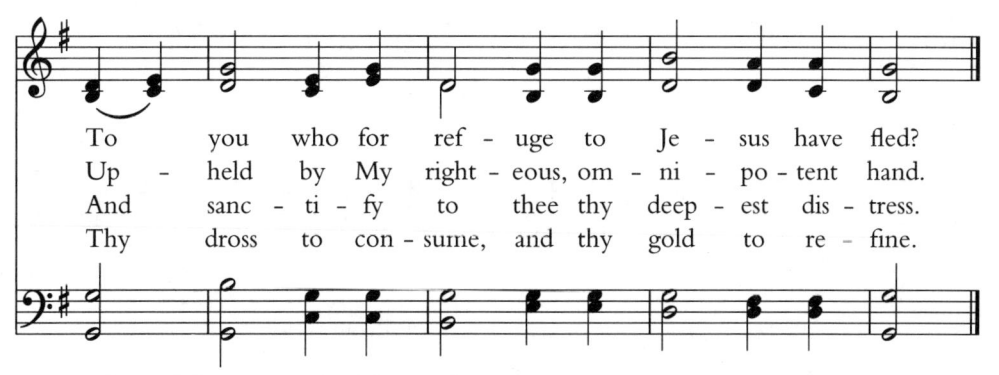

To you who for refuge to Jesus have fled?
Upheld by My righteous, omnipotent hand.
And sanctify to thee thy deepest distress.
Thy dross to consume, and thy gold to refine.

5. "The soul that on Jesus hath leaned for repose,
I will not, I will not desert to its foes;
That soul, though all hell should endeavor to shake,
I'll never, no, never, no, never forsake."

LIFE IN CHRIST

68 I'm Gonna Live So God Can Use Me

I'M GONNA LIVE   Irregular

African-American spiritual

African-American spiritual
arr. Wendell Whalum (1932–1987)

1. I'm gonna live so (live so) God can use me
2. I'm gonna work so (work so) God can use me
3. I'm gonna pray so (pray so) God can use me
4. I'm gonna sing so (sing so) God can use me

Anywhere, Lord, anytime! (anytime!)

I'm gonna live so (live so) God can use me
work so (work so)
pray so (pray so)
sing so (sing so)

Anywhere, Lord, anytime!
(my Lord,) (anytime!)

Music: arrangement © by the estate of Wendell Whalum. Used by permission.

Just As I Am, without One Plea

69

LIFE IN CHRIST

WOODWORTH L.M.

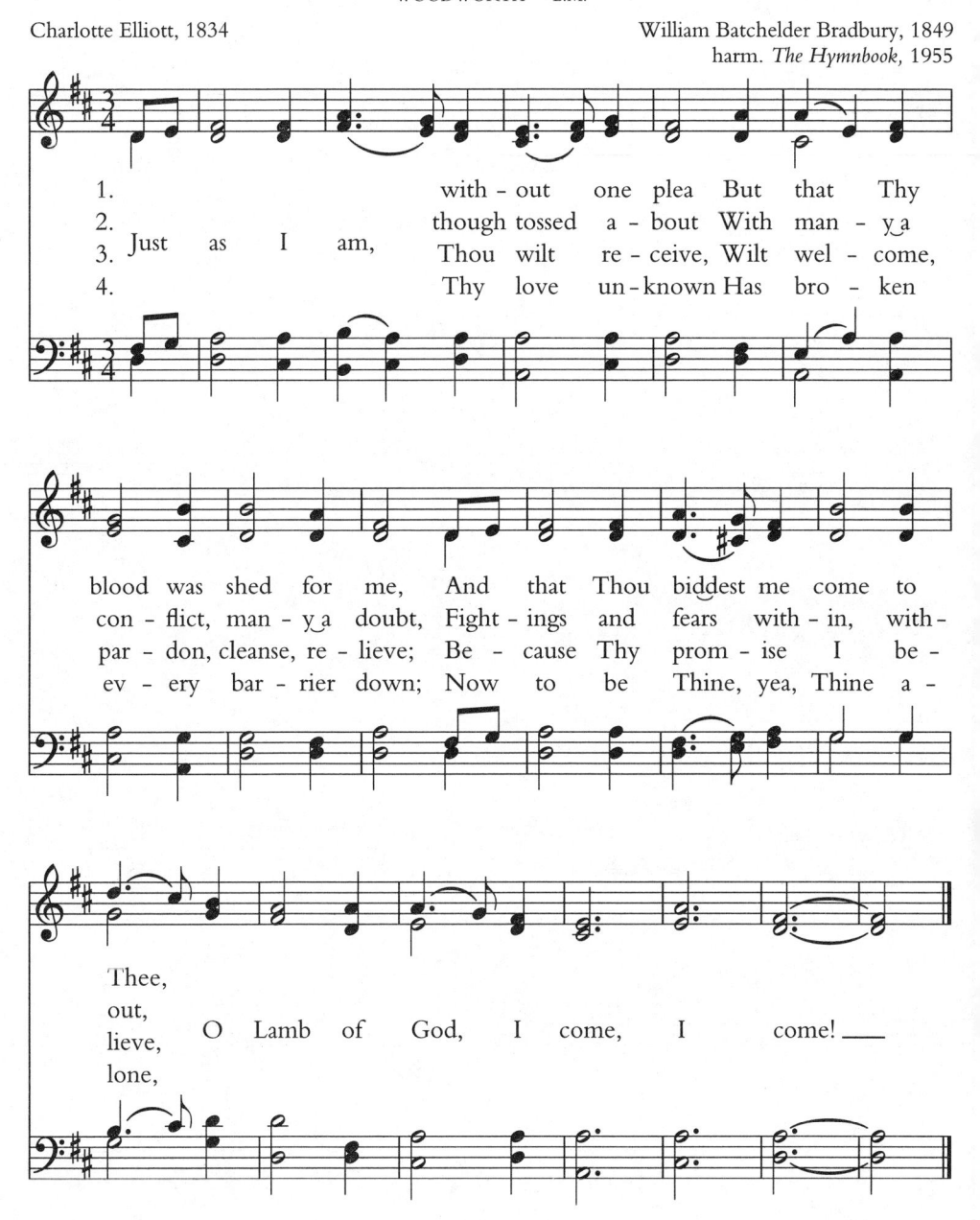

Charlotte Elliott, 1834

William Batchelder Bradbury, 1849
harm. *The Hymnbook,* 1955

1. Just as I am, without one plea But that Thy blood was shed for me, And that Thou biddest me come to Thee,
2. Just as I am, though tossed about With many a conflict, many a doubt, Fightings and fears within, without,
3. Just as I am, Thou wilt receive, Wilt welcome, pardon, cleanse, relieve; Because Thy promise I believe,
4. Just as I am, Thy love unknown Has broken every barrier down; Now to be Thine, yea, Thine alone,

O Lamb of God, I come, I come!

Music: harmonization copyright MCMLV by John Ribble; renewed 1983; from *The Hymnbook,* published by Westminster Press.

LIFE IN CHRIST

70 Lord, I Want to Be a Christian

I WANT TO BE A CHRISTIAN   Irregular

African-American spiritual   African-American spiritual

1. Lord, I want to be a Christian in-a my heart, in-a my heart,
2. Lord, I want to be more loving in-a my heart, in-a my heart,
3. Lord, I want to be more holy in-a my heart, in-a my heart,
4. Lord, I want to be like Jesus in-a my heart, in-a my heart,

Lord, I want to be a Christian in-a my heart.
Lord, I want to be more loving in-a my heart.
Lord, I want to be more holy in-a my heart.
Lord, I want to be like Jesus in-a my heart.

In-a my heart, In-a my heart,
(In-a my heart,)   (In-a my heart,)

Lord, I want to be a Christian in-a my heart.
Lord, I want to be more loving in-a my heart.
Lord, I want to be more holy in-a my heart.
Lord, I want to be like Jesus in-a my heart.

LIFE IN CHRIST

My Hope Is Built on Nothing Less 71
SOLID ROCK L.M. with Refrain

Edward Mote, c. 1834 — William Batchelder Bradbury, 1863

1. My hope is built on nothing less Than Jesus' blood and righteousness; I dare not trust the sweetest frame, But wholly lean on Jesus' name.
2. When darkness veils His lovely face, I rest on His unchanging grace; In every high and stormy gale, My anchor holds within the veil.
3. His oath, His covenant, His blood Support me in the whelming flood; When all around my soul gives way, He then is all my hope and stay.
4. When He shall come with trumpet sound, O may I then in Him be found, Dressed in His righteousness alone, Faultless to stand before the throne.

Refrain
On Christ, the solid Rock, I stand; All other ground is sinking sand, All other ground is sinking sand.

LIFE IN CHRIST

72 Love Divine, All Loves Excelling
HYFRYDOL 8.7.8.7.D

Charles Wesley, 1747 Rowland Hugh Prichard, 1831

1. Love divine, all loves excelling,
Joy of heaven, to earth come down,
Fix in us Thy humble dwelling,
All Thy faithful mercies crown!
Jesus, Thou art

2. Breathe, O breathe Thy loving Spirit
Into every troubled breast!
Let us all in Thee inherit,
Let us find the promised rest;
Take away the

3. Come, Almighty to deliver,
Let us all Thy life receive;
Suddenly return, and never,
Nevermore Thy temples leave.
Thee we would be

4. Finish, then, Thy new creation;
Pure and spotless let us be;
Let us see Thy great salvation
Perfectly restored in Thee;
Changed from glory

LIFE IN CHRIST

all com-pass-ion, Pure, un-bound-ed love Thou
love of sin-ning; Al-pha and O-me-ga
al-ways bless-ing, Serve Thee as Thy hosts a-
in-to glo-ry, Till in heaven we take our

art; Vis-it us with Thy sal-
be; End of faith, as its be-
bove; Pray, and praise Thee with-out
place, Till we cast our crowns be-

va-tion, En-ter ev-ery trem-bling heart.
gin-ning, Set our hearts at lib-er-ty.
ceas-ing, Glo-ry in Thy per-fect love.
fore Thee, Lost in won-der, love, and praise.

LIFE IN CHRIST

73 Somebody's Knocking at Your Door
SOMEBODY'S KNOCKIN'   Irregular

African-American spiritual

African-American spiritual
arr. Joy F. Patterson, 1989

Some-bod-y's knock-ing at your door; Some-bod-y's knock-ing at your door; O sin-ner, why don't you an-swer? Some-bod-y's knock-ing at your door.

1. Knocks like Je-sus,
2. Can't you hear Him? Some-bod-y's knock-ing at your door;
3. An-swer Je-sus.

Music: arrangement © 1990 Joy F. Patterson. All rights reserved. Used by permission.

LIFE IN CHRIST

Knocks like Jesus,
Can't you hear Him? Somebody's knocking at your door,
Answer Jesus.

O sinner, why don't you answer? Somebody's knocking at your door.

LIFE IN CHRIST

74 My Faith Looks Up to Thee
OLIVET 6.6.4.6.6.6.4

Ray Palmer, 1830   Lowell Mason, 1831

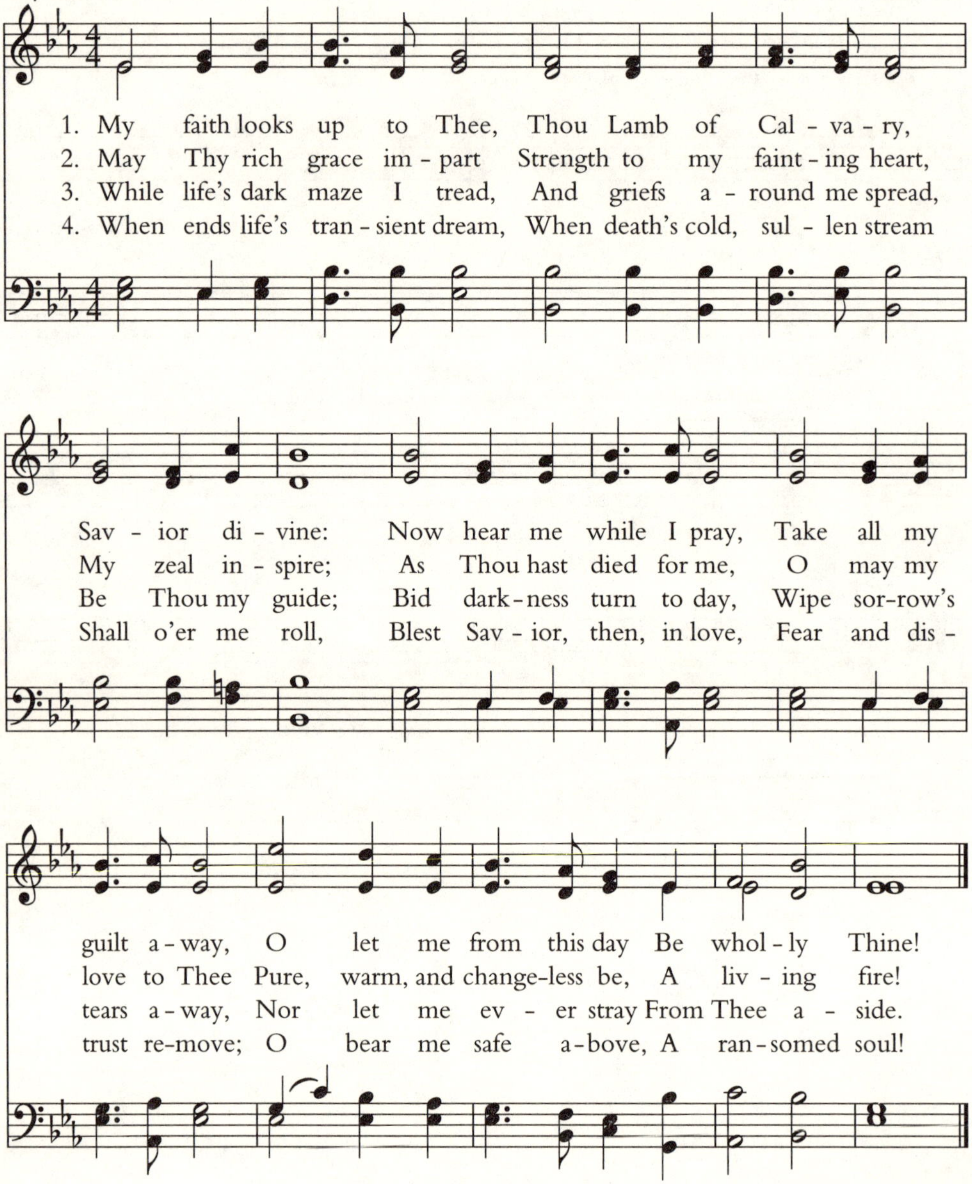

1. My faith looks up to Thee, Thou Lamb of Cal-va-ry, Sav-ior di-vine: Now hear me while I pray, Take all my guilt a-way, O let me from this day Be whol-ly Thine!
2. May Thy rich grace im-part Strength to my faint-ing heart, My zeal in-spire; As Thou hast died for me, O may my love to Thee Pure, warm, and change-less be, A liv-ing fire!
3. While life's dark maze I tread, And griefs a-round me spread, Be Thou my guide; Bid dark-ness turn to day, Wipe sorrow's tears a-way, Nor let me ev-er stray From Thee a-side.
4. When ends life's tran-sient dream, When death's cold, sul-len stream Shall o'er me roll, Blest Sav-ior, then, in love, Fear and dis-trust re-move; O bear me safe a-bove, A ran-somed soul!

LIFE IN CHRIST

O Love That Wilt Not Let Me Go 75
ST. MARGARET 8.8.8.8.8.6

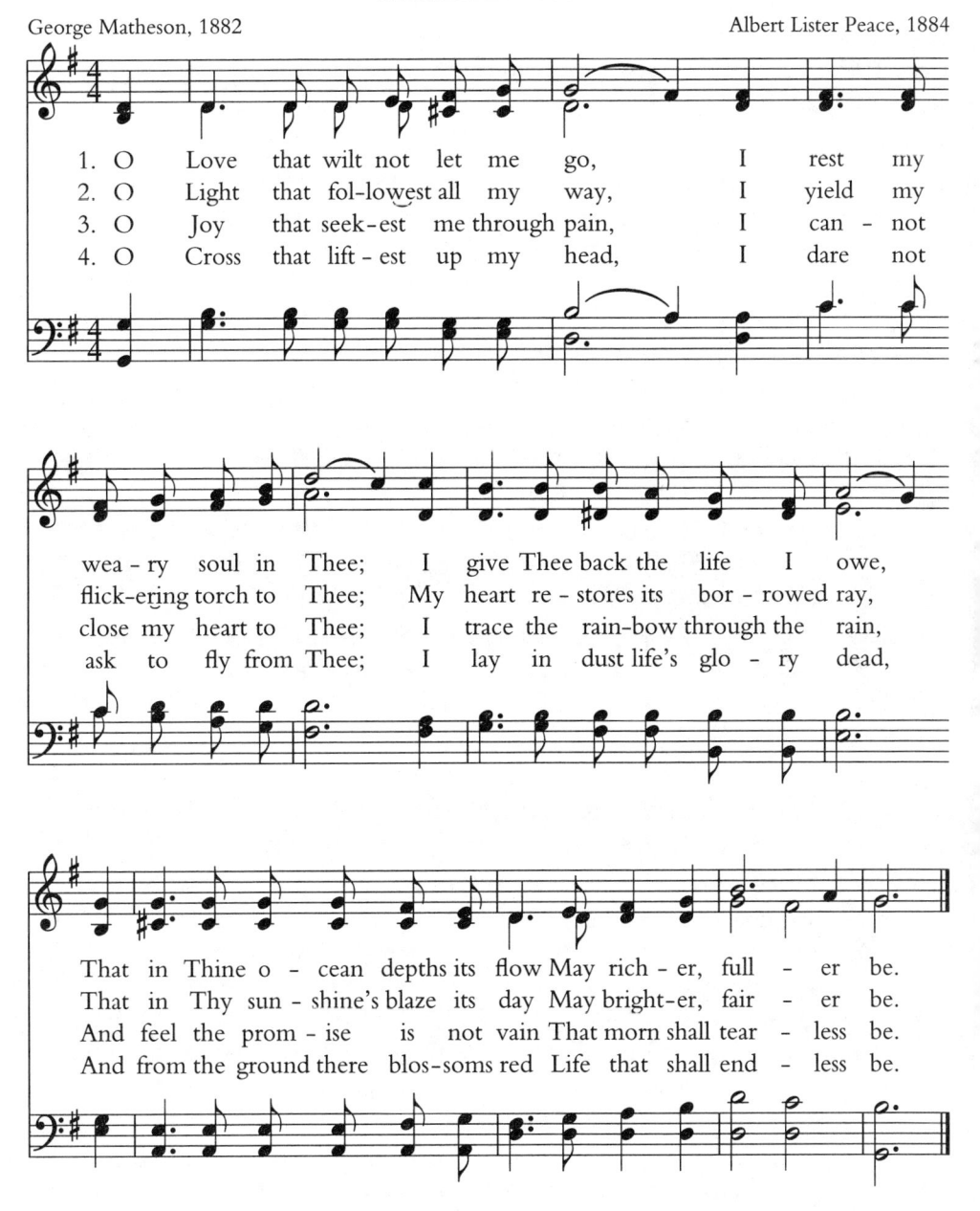

George Matheson, 1882   Albert Lister Peace, 1884

1. O Love that wilt not let me go, I rest my weary soul in Thee; I give Thee back the life I owe, That in Thine ocean depths its flow May richer, fuller be.

2. O Light that followest all my way, I yield my flickering torch to Thee; My heart restores its borrowed ray, That in Thy sunshine's blaze its day May brighter, fairer be.

3. O Joy that seekest me through pain, I cannot close my heart to Thee; I trace the rainbow through the rain, And feel the promise is not vain That morn shall tearless be.

4. O Cross that liftest up my head, I dare not ask to fly from Thee; I lay in dust life's glory dead, And from the ground there blossoms red Life that shall endless be.

LIFE IN CHRIST

76. Savior, Like a Shepherd Lead Us

BRADBURY 8.7.8.7.D

Thrupp's *Hymns for the Young*, 1836
William Batchelder Bradbury, 1859

1. Savior, like a shepherd lead us, Much we need Thy tender care;
In Thy pleasant pastures feed us, For our use Thy folds prepare:
Blessed Jesus, blessed Jesus, Thou hast bought us, Thine we are;
Blessed Jesus, blessed Jesus, Thou hast bought us, Thine we are.

2. Thou hast promised to receive us, Poor and sinful though we be;
Thou hast mercy to relieve us, Grace to cleanse, and power to free:
Blessed Jesus, blessed Jesus, Early let us turn to Thee;
Blessed Jesus, blessed Jesus, Early let us turn to Thee.

3. Early let us seek Thy favor; Early let us do Thy will;
Blessed Lord and only Savior, With Thy love our bosoms fill:
Blessed Jesus, blessed Jesus, Thou hast loved us, love us still;
Blessed Jesus, blessed Jesus, Thou hast loved us, love us still.

Take My Life

HENDON 7.7.7.7

Frances Ridley Havergal, 1874 — H. A. César Malan, 1827

1. Take my life, and let it be Consecrated, Lord, to Thee. Take my moments and my days; Let them flow in ceaseless praise, Let them flow in ceaseless praise.

2. Take my hands, and let them move At the impulse of Thy love. Take my feet, and let them be Swift and beautiful for Thee, Swift and beautiful for Thee.

3. Take my voice, and let me sing, Always, only, for my King. Take my lips, and let them be Filled with messages from Thee, Filled with messages from Thee.

4. Take my silver and my gold, Not a mite would I withhold; Take my intellect, and use Every power as Thou shalt choose, Every power as Thou shalt choose.

5. Take my will, and make it Thine; It shall be no longer mine. Take my heart, it is Thine own; It shall be Thy royal throne, It shall be Thy royal throne.

6. Take my love; my Lord, I pour At Thy feet its treasure store. Take myself, and I will be Ever, only, all for Thee, Ever, only, all for Thee.

LIFE IN CHRIST

78 There Is a Balm in Gilead
BALM IN GILEAD 7.6.7.6 with Refrain

African-American spiritual

African-American spiritual
arr. Melva W. Costen, 1989; alt.

There is a balm in Gil-e-ad to make the wound-ed whole.

There is a balm in Gil-e-ad to heal the sin-sick soul. *Fine*

1. Some-times I feel dis-cour-aged, And think my work's in vain,
2. Don't ev-er feel dis-cour-aged, For Je-sus is your friend,
3. If you can-not preach like Pe-ter, If you can-not pray like Paul,

But then the Ho-ly Spir-it Re-vives my soul a-gain. *D.C.*
And if you lack for knowl-edge He'll not re-fuse to lend.
You can tell the love of Je-sus And say, "He died for all."

Music: arrangement © 1990 Melva W. Costen. All rights reserved. Used by permission.

LIFE IN CHRIST

Precious Lord, Take My Hand   79
PRECIOUS LORD   6.6.9.D

Thomas A. Dorsey, 1938

George N. Allen, 1844
arr. Thomas A. Dorsey, 1938

1. Pre-cious Lord, take my hand, Lead me on, help me stand; I am tired, I am weak, I am worn; Through the storm, through the night, Lead me on to the light; Take my hand, pre-cious Lord, lead me home.

2. When my way grows drear, Pre-cious Lord, lin-ger near; When my life is al-most gone, Hear my cry, hear my call, Hold my hand lest I fall; Take my hand, pre-cious Lord, lead me home.

Text and Music: copyright © 1938 by Hill & Range Songs, Inc. Copyright renewed, assigned to Unichappell Music, Inc. (Rightsong Music, Publisher). International copyright secured. All rights reserved. Used by permission.

LIFE IN CHRIST

80 Jin Shil Ha Shin Chin Goo
What a Friend We Have in Jesus
CONVERSE 8.7.8.7.D

Joseph Scriven, c. 1855
transliteration of Korean: Myung Ja Yue

Charles Crozat Converse, 1868

1. Chway jim ma tun oo ree goo joo Uh jjee joh un chin goon jee
2. She hum guhk juhng mo dun kway rom Um nun sah rahm noo goon gah

1. What a friend we have in Je-sus, All our sins and griefs to bear!
2. Have we tri-als and temp-ta-tions? Is there trou-ble an-y-where?

Kuhk juhng keun shim moo guh oon jim Oo ree joo ggeh mat ggee seh
Boo jil up see nahk shim mahl go Kee doh duh ryuh ah ray seh

What a priv-i-lege to car-ry Ev-ery-thing to God in prayer!
We should nev-er be dis-cour-aged: Take it to the Lord in prayer!

Joo ggeh sah juhng ah ray jahn ah Pyung wha uht jee mot ha neh
Ee run jin shil ha shin chin goo Uh dee dah shi iss ul ggah

Oh, what peace we of-ten for-feit, Oh, what need-less pain we bear,
Can we find a friend so faith-ful, Who will all our sor-rows share?

Text: transliteration © 1990 Westminster/John Knox Press. All rights reserved.

LIFE IN CHRIST

Oo ree du ree uht jjee ha yuh	Ah rel joo rul mo rul kka
Oo ree yak ham ah shi oh nee	Uh jjee ah nee ah rel kka
All be-cause we do not car-ry	Ev-ery-thing to God in prayer!
Je-sus knows our ev-ery weak-ness;	Take it to the Lord in prayer!

3. Kuhn shim guhk juhng moo guh ooh jim
   Ah nee jin jah noo goon gah
   Pee nahn chuh nun oo ree Ye su
   Joo ggeh kee doh duh ree seh
   Seh sahng chin goo myul see ha go
   Nuh rul joh rong ha yuh doh
   Joo eh poo meh ahn gee uh suh
   Cham dwen wee ro baat get neh.

3. Are we weak and heavy laden,
   Cumbered with a load of care?
   Precious Savior, still our refuge—
   Take it to the Lord in prayer!
   Do thy friends despise, forsake thee?
   Take it to the Lord in prayer!
   In His arms He'll take and shield thee,
   Thou wilt find a solace there.

LIFE IN CHRIST

81 My Jesus, I Love Thee
GORDON 11.11.11.11

William R. Featherstone, 1864

Adoniram J. Gordon, 1894
harm. alt., 1953

1. My Jesus, I love Thee, I know Thou art mine;
2. I love Thee, because Thou hast first loved me
3. In mansions of glory and endless delight

For Thee all the follies of sin I resign;
And purchased my pardon on Calvary's tree.
I'll ever adore Thee in heaven so bright;

My gracious Redeemer, my Savior art Thou;
I love Thee for wearing the thorns on Thy brow;
I'll sing with the glittering crown on my brow;

If ever I loved Thee, my Jesus, 'tis now. A-men.

LIFE IN CHRIST

Ten Thousand Times Ten Thousand 82
ALFORD 7.6.8.6.D

Henry Alford, 1867, alt.   John B. Dykes, 1875

1. Ten thou-sand times ten thou-sand In spar-kling rai-ment bright,
   The ar-mies of the ran-somed saints Throng up the steeps of light;
   'Tis fin-ished, all is fin-ished, Their fight with death and sin:
   Fling o-pen wide the gold-en gates, And let the vic-tors in.

2. What rush of al-le-lu-ias Fills all the earth and sky!
   What ring-ing of a thou-sand harps Be-speaks the tri-umph nigh!
   O day, for which cre-a-tion And all its tribes were made;
   O joy, for all its for-mer woes A thou-sand-fold re-paid!

3. O then what rap-tured greet-ings On Ca-naan's hap-py shore;
   What meet-ing there of part-ed friends Where part-ings are no more!
   Then eyes with joy shall spar-kle, That brimmed with tears of late;
   Or-phans no long-er fa-ther-less, Nor wid-ows des-o-late.

4. Bring near Thy great sal-va-tion, Thou Lamb for sin-ners slain;
   Fill up the roll of Thine e-lect, Then take Thy power, and reign;
   Ap-pear, De-sire of na-tions, Thine ex-iles long for home;
   Show in the heaven Thy prom-ised sign; Thou Prince and Sav-ior, come. A-men.

LIFE IN CHRIST

83   Living for Jesus a Life That Is True
LIVING   10.10.10.10 with Refrain

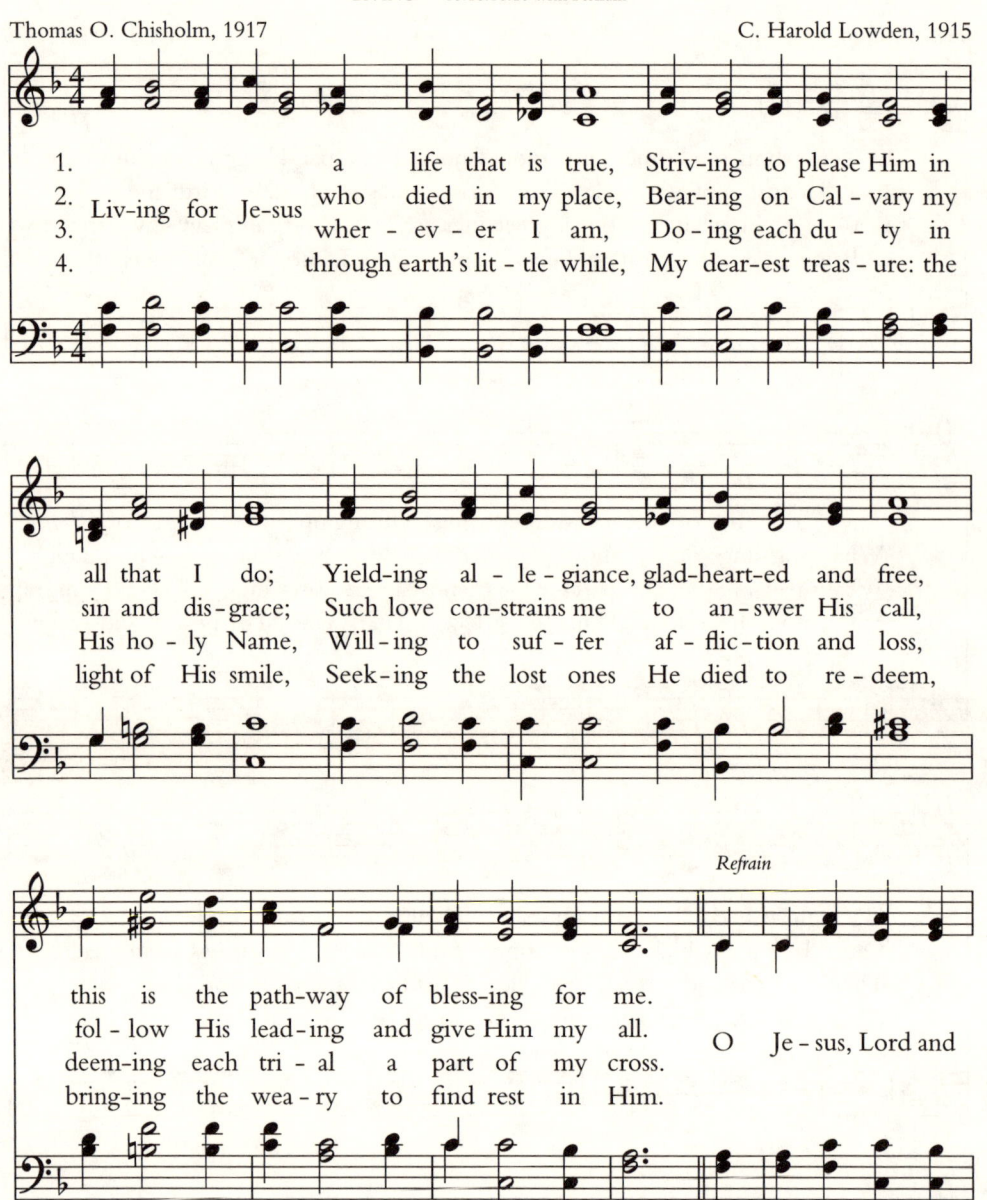

Thomas O. Chisholm, 1917   C. Harold Lowden, 1915

1. Living for Jesus a life that is true, Striving to please Him in all that I do; Yielding allegiance, glad-hearted and free, this is the pathway of blessing for me.
2. Living for Jesus who died in my place, Bearing on Calvary my sin and disgrace; Such love constrains me to answer His call, follow His leading and give Him my all.
3. Living for Jesus wherever I am, Doing each duty in His holy Name, Willing to suffer affliction and loss, deeming each trial a part of my cross.
4. Living for Jesus through earth's little while, My dearest treasure: the light of His smile, Seeking the lost ones He died to redeem, bringing the weary to find rest in Him.

Refrain

O Jesus, Lord and

Text and Music: © 1917 Heidelberg Press, © renewed 1945 C. Harold Lowden. Assigned to The Rodeheaver Co. (A Div. of Word, Inc.)

LIFE IN CHRIST

Savior, I give myself to Thee, For Thou, in Thy atonement, didst give Thyself for me; I own no other Master, My heart shall be Thy throne; My life I give, henceforth to live, O Christ, for Thee alone.

LIFE IN CHRIST

84   I Have Decided to Follow Jesus
ASSAM Irregular

Anonymous   Anonymous

1. I have de-cid-ed to fol-low Je-sus, I have de-cid-ed to fol-low Je-sus, I have de-cid-ed to fol-low Je-sus—
2. The world be-hind me, the cross be-fore me, The world be-hind me, the cross be-fore me, The world be-hind me, the cross be-fore me—
3. Though none go with me, I still will fol-low, Though none go with me, I still will fol-low, Though none go with me, I still will fol-low—
4. Will you de-cide now to fol-low Je-sus? Will you de-cide now to fol-low Je-sus? Will you de-cide now to fol-low Je-sus?—

No turn-ing back, no turn-ing back.

LIFE IN CHRIST

We Would See Jesus 85
CUSHMAN 11.10.11.10

J. Edgar Park, 1913
Herbert B. Turner, 1907

1. We would see Jesus, lo! His star is shining
2. We would see Jesus, Mary's Son most holy,
3. We would see Jesus, on the mountain teaching,
4. We would see Jesus, in His work of healing,
5. We would see Jesus, in the early morning,

Above the stable while the angels sing;
Light of the village life from day to day;
With all the listening people gathered round;
At eventide before the sun was set;
Still as of old He calleth, "Follow me!"

There in a manger on the hay reclining;
Shining revealed through every task most lowly,
While birds and flowers and sky above are preaching
Divine and human, in His deep revealing
Let us arise, all meaner service scorning;

Haste, let us lay our gifts before the King.
The Christ of God, the Life, the Truth, the Way.
The blessedness which simple trust has found.
Of God made flesh, in loving service met.
Lord, we are Thine, we give ourselves to Thee.

LIFE IN CHRIST

86 Just a Closer Walk with Thee
CLOSER WALK   Irregular

Unknown

Traditional
arr. by Kenneth Morris, 1916

Refrain

Just a clo-ser walk with Thee; Grant it, Je-sus, if you please,
Dai-ly walk-ing close with Thee, Let it be, dear Lord, let it be.

Fine

1. I am weak, but Thou art strong; Je-sus, keep me from all wrong.
2. Through this world of toils and snares, If I fal-ter, Lord, who cares?
3. When my feeb-le life is o'er, Times for me won't be no more.

I'll be sat-is-fied as long As I walk, let me walk close with Thee.
Who with me my bur-dens shares? None but Thee, dear Lord, none but Thee.
Guide me gent-ly, safe-ly o'er, To Thy king-dom shore, to Thy shore.

D.C.

Note: Slow for solo, spiritually for chorus

Music: arr. copyrighted 1940 by Kenneth Morris. Used by permission.

CHURCH

God of Grace and God of Glory
87

CWM RHONDDA 8.7.8.7.8.7.7

Harry Emerson Fosdick, 1930, alt.   John Hughes, 1907

1. God of grace and God of glory, On Thy people pour Thy power; Crown Thine an-cient church's sto-ry; Bring its bud to glo-rious flower. Grant us wis-dom, grant us cour-age For the fac-ing of this hour, For the fac-ing of this hour.

2. Lo! the hosts of e-vil round us Scorn Thy Christ, as-sail Thy ways! From the fears that long have bound us Free our hearts to faith and praise. Grant us wis-dom, grant us cour-age For the liv-ing of these days, For the liv-ing of these days.

3. Cure Thy chil-dren's war-ring mad-ness, Bend our pride to Thy con-trol; Shame our wan-ton, self-ish glad-ness, Rich in things and poor in soul. Grant us wis-dom, grant us cour-age Lest we miss Thy king-dom's goal, Lest we miss Thy king-dom's goal.

4. Set our feet on loft-y pla-ces; Gird our lives that they may be Ar-mored with all Christ-like gra-ces, Pledged to set all cap-tives free. Grant us wis-dom, grant us cour-age That we fail not them nor Thee! That we fail not them nor Thee!

Text: used by permission of Elinor Fosdick Downs.

CHURCH

88 Rescue the Perishing
RESCUE 6.5.10.D

Fanny J. Crosby, 1869   *William H. Doane, 1870*

1. Res-cue the per-ish-ing, care for the dy-ing,
2. Though they are slight-ing Him, still He is wait-ing,
3. Down in the hu-man heart, crushed by the tempt-er,
4. Res-cue the per-ish-ing, du-ty de-mands it;

Snatch them in pit-y from sin and the grave;
Wait-ing the pen-i-tent child to re-ceive;
Feel-ings lie bur-ied that grace can re-store;
Strength for thy la-bor the Lord will pro-vide;

Weep o'er the err-ing one, lift up the fall-en,
Plead with them ear-nest-ly, plead with them gent-ly;
Touched by a lov-ing heart, wak-ened by kind-ness,
Back to the nar-row way pa-tient-ly win them;

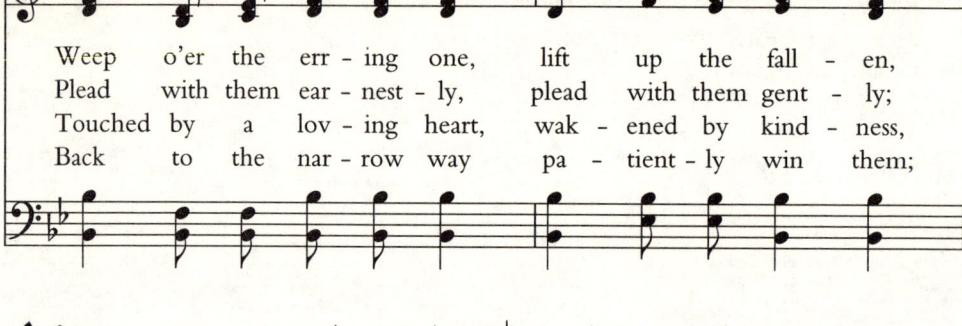

Tell them of Je-sus, the might-y to save.
He will for-give if they on-ly be-lieve.
Chords that were bro-ken will vi-brate once more.
Tell the poor wan-derer a Sav-ior has died.

Refrain

Rescue the perishing, care for the dying,
Jesus is merciful, Jesus will save.

Blest Be the Tie That Binds   89
DENNIS SM

John Fawcett, 1782

Johann Georg Nägeli (1773–1836)
arr. Lowell Mason, 1845

1. Blest be the tie that binds Our hearts in Christian love:
2. Before our *Father's throne We pour our ardent prayers;
3. We share our mutual woes. Our mutual burdens bear,
4. From sorrow, toil, and pain, And sin we shall be free;

The fellowship of kindred minds Is like to that above.
Our fears, our hopes, our aims are one. Our comforts and our cares.
And often for each other flows The sympathizing tear.
And perfect love and friendship reign Through all eternity.

*or Maker's

90. We've a Story to Tell to the Nations

MESSAGE 10.8.8.7. with Refrain

H. Ernest Nichol, 1896

1. We've a story to tell to the nations,
That shall turn their hearts to the right,
A story of truth and mercy,
A story of peace and light,
A story of peace and light.

2. We've a song to be sung to the nations,
That shall lift their hearts to the Lord,
A song that shall conquer evil
And shatter the spear and sword,
And shatter the spear and sword.

3. We've a message to give to the nations,
That the Lord Who reigneth above
Hath sent us His Son to save us,
And show us that God is love,
And show us that God is love.

4. We've a Savior to show to the nations,
Who the path of sorrow hath trod,
That all of the world's great peoples
Might come to the truth of God,
Might come to the truth of God.

CHURCH

Refrain

For the darkness shall turn to dawning, And the dawning to noonday bright; And Christ's great kingdom shall come on earth, The kingdom of love and light.

CHURCH

91 The Church's One Foundation
AURELIA 7.6.7.6.D

Samuel John Stone, 1866, alt.
Samuel Sebastian Wesley, 1864

1. The church's one foundation Is Jesus Christ her Lord;
   She is His new creation By water and the word;
   From heaven He came and sought her To be His holy bride;
   With His own blood He bought her, And for her life He died.

2. Elect from every nation, Yet one o'er all the earth,
   Her charter of salvation One Lord, one faith, one birth;
   One holy name she blesses, Partakes one holy food,
   And to one hope she presses, With every grace endued.

3. Though with a scornful wonder This world sees her oppressed,
   By schisms rent asunder, By heresies distressed,
   Yet saints their watch are keeping; Their cry goes up: "How long?"
   And soon the night of weeping Shall be the morn of song.

4. Mid toil and tribulation, And tumult of her war,
   She waits the consummation Of peace forevermore;
   Till with the vision glorious Her longing eyes are blest,
   And the great church victorious Shall be the church at rest.

5. Yet she on earth has union   O happy ones and holy!
   With God the Three in One,   Lord, give us grace that we,
   And mystic sweet communion   Like them, the meek and lowly,
   With those whose rest is won: May live eternally.

Great Day!

Irregular

CHURCH
92

African-American spiritual

African-American spiritual
arr. Joseph T. Jones (1902–1983)
adapt. Melva W. Costen, 1989

Great day! Great day, the right-eous march-ing, Great day! God's going to build up Zi-on's walls. Oh, Zi-on's walls.

1. The char-i-ot rode on the moun-tain-top, God's going to build up Zi-on's walls. My God spoke and the char-i-ot did stop. God's going to build up Zi-on's walls. Oh,

2. This is the day of Ju-bi-lee, God's going to build up Zi-on's walls. God shall set the peo-ple free. God's going to build up Zi-on's walls. Oh,

Music: adaptation © 1990 Melva W. Costen. All rights reserved. Used by permission.

CHURCH

93 Lead On, O King Eternal
LANCASHIRE 7.6.7.6.D

Ernest W. Shurtleff, 1888
Henry Thomas Smart, c. 1835

1.   The day of march has come;
2. Lead on, O King e-ter-nal, Till sin's fierce war shall cease,
3.   We fol-low, not with fears;

Hence-forth in fields of con-quest Thy tents shall be our home:
And ho-li-ness shall whis-per The sweet a-men of peace;
For glad-ness breaks like morn-ing Wher-e'er Thy face ap-pears;

Through days of prep-a-ra-tion Thy grace has made us strong,
For not with swords' loud clash-ing, Nor roll of stir-ring drums;
Thy cross is lift-ed o'er us; We jour-ney in its light:

And now, O King e-ter-nal, We lift our bat-tle song.
With deeds of love and mer-cy The heaven-ly king-dom comes.
The crown a-waits the con-quest; Lead on, O God of might.

CHURCH

My Lord! What a Morning
Irregular

African-American spiritual

African-American spiritual
arr. Melva W. Costen, 1989

94

Refrain

My Lord! what a morn-ing, My Lord! what a morn-ing,

Oh, my Lord! what a morn-ing, When the stars be-gin to

fall, When the stars be-gin to fall.
1. You will hear the trum-pet
2. You will hear the sin-ner
3. You will hear the Chris-tian

sound
cry   To wake the na-tions un-der-ground,
shout

D.C.

Look-ing to my God's right hand When the stars be-gin to fall.

Music: arrangement © 1990 Melva W. Costen. All rights reserved. Used by permission.

MORNING AND OPENING HYMNS

95 Praise Ye the Lord, the Almighty
LOBE DEN HERREN 14.14.4.7.8

Joachim Neander, 1680
trans. Catherine Winkworth, 1863, alt.

Stralsund *Ernewerten Gesangbuch*, 1665
harm. *The Chorale Book for England*, 1863
desc. Craig Sellar Lang, 1953

3. Praise ye the Lord! Oh, let all that is in me adore Him! All that hath life and breath, come now with

1. Praise ye the Lord, the Almighty, the King of creation! O my soul, praise Him, for He is thy
2. Praise ye the Lord, who o'er all things so wondrously reigneth, Shelters thee under His wings, yea, so
3. Praise ye the Lord! Oh, let all that is in me adore Him! All that hath life and breath, come now with

Music: descant © Novello & Co. LTD. 1955

MORNING AND OPENING HYMNS

MORNING AND OPENING HYMNS

96 How Great Thou Art

O STORE GUD 11.10.11.10 with Refrain

Carl Gustav Boberg, 1855
English version: Stuart K. Hine, 1953
transliteration of Korean: Myung Ja Yue, 1989

Swedish folk melody
harm. Stuart K. Hine, 1949

1. Joo ha nah nim jee eu shin mo dun seh geh Nae ma um
2. Soop sok ee nah hum hahn sahn gol jjak eh suh Jee juh gee

1. O Lord my God! when I in awe-some won-der Con-sid-er
2. When through the woods and for-est glades I wan-der And hear the

so geh geu ree uh bol ttae Ha neul eh byul ool
nun juh sae so ree deul gwa Ko yo ha geh heu

all the *worlds Thy hands have made, I see the stars, I
birds sing sweet-ly in the trees; When I look down from

lyuh paw jee nun nweh sung Joo nim eh kwon nung oo joo eh chan
reu nun see nae moo reun Joo nim eh som ssee no rae ha doh

hear the *roll-ing thun-der, Thy power through-out the u-ni-verse dis-
loft-y moun-tain gran-deur And hear the brook and feel the gen-tle

*Note: Original English words were "works" and "mighty."

Music: harmonization © Copyright 1953 S. K. Hine. Assigned to Manna Music, Inc., 35255 Brooten Road, Pacific City, OR 97135. Renewed 1981. All rights reserved. Used by permission (ASCAP).

MORNING AND OPENING HYMNS

Hooryum
Refrain

neh / dah Joo nim eh nop go wee dae ha shim ul
played: / breeze: Then sings my soul, my Sav-ior God, to Thee,

Nae young hon ee chan yahng ha neh Joo nim eh nop go
How great Thou art, how great Thou art! Then sings my soul, my

wee dae ha shim eul Nae young hon ee chan yahng ha neh
Sav-ior God, to Thee, How great Thou art, how great Thou art!

3. Joo ha nah nim tok seng ja ak kim up see
   Oo ree rul wee hae ddang eh bo nae uh
   Seep ja ga eh pee heul lyuh juk keh ha sa
   Nae mo dun chway rul goo sok ha shun neh
   Hooryum

3. And when I think that God, His Son not sparing,
   Sent Him to die, I scarce can take it in;
   That on the cross, my burden gladly bearing,
   He bled and died to take away my sin:
   Refrain

4. Nae joo Ye su seh sahng eh dah see ol ttae
   Juh chun goo geu ro nal in doh ha ree
   Na kyum son hee up deu ryuh kyung bae ha myuh
   Young won hee joo rul chan yahng ha ree rah
   Hooryum

4. When Christ shall come with shout of acclamation
   And take me home, what joy shall fill my heart!
   Then I shall bow in humble adoration,
   And there proclaim, my God, how great Thou art!
   Refrain

MORNING AND OPENING HYMNS

97 I Greet Thee, Who My Sure Redeemer Art
TOULON 10.10.10.10

attr. John Calvin
French Psalter, Strassburg, 1545
trans. Elizabeth Lee Smith, 1868

adapt. from Genevan 124
Genevan Psalter, 1551

1. I greet Thee, Who my sure Re-deem-er art,
   My on-ly trust and Sav-ior of my heart,
   Who pain didst un-der-go for my poor sake;
   I pray Thee from our hearts all cares to take.

2. Thou art the King of mer-cy and of grace,
   Reign-ing om-nip-o-tent in ev-ery place:
   So come, O King, and our whole be-ing sway;
   Shine on us with the light of Thy pure day.

3. Thou art the life, by which a-lone we live,
   And all our sub-stance and our strength re-ceive;
   Sus-tain us by Thy faith and by Thy power,
   And give us strength in ev-ery try-ing hour.

4. Thou hast the true and per-fect gen-tle-ness,
   No harsh-ness hast Thou and no bit-ter-ness:
   O grant to us the grace we find in Thee,
   That we may dwell in per-fect u-ni-ty.

5. Our hope is in no other save in Thee;
   Our faith is built upon Thy promise free;
   Lord, give us peace, and make us calm and sure,
   That in Thy strength we evermore endure.

Morning Has Broken

98

BUNESSAN 5.5.5.4.D

Eleanor Farjeon, 1931

Gaelic melody
arr. Dale Grotenhuis, 1985

1. Morning has broken like the first morning, Blackbird has spoken like the first bird. Praise for the singing! Praise for the morning! Praise for them, springing fresh from the Word!
2. Sweet the rain's new fall sunlit from heaven, Like the first dewfall on the first grass. Praise for the sweetness of the wet garden, Sprung in completeness where God's feet pass.
3. Mine is the sunlight! Mine is the morning Born of the One Light Eden saw play! Praise with elation, praise every morning God's re-creation of the new day!

Music: arrangement Dale Grotenhuis © 1987, CRC Publications, Grand Rapids, MI 49560. All rights reserved.

MORNING AND OPENING HYMNS

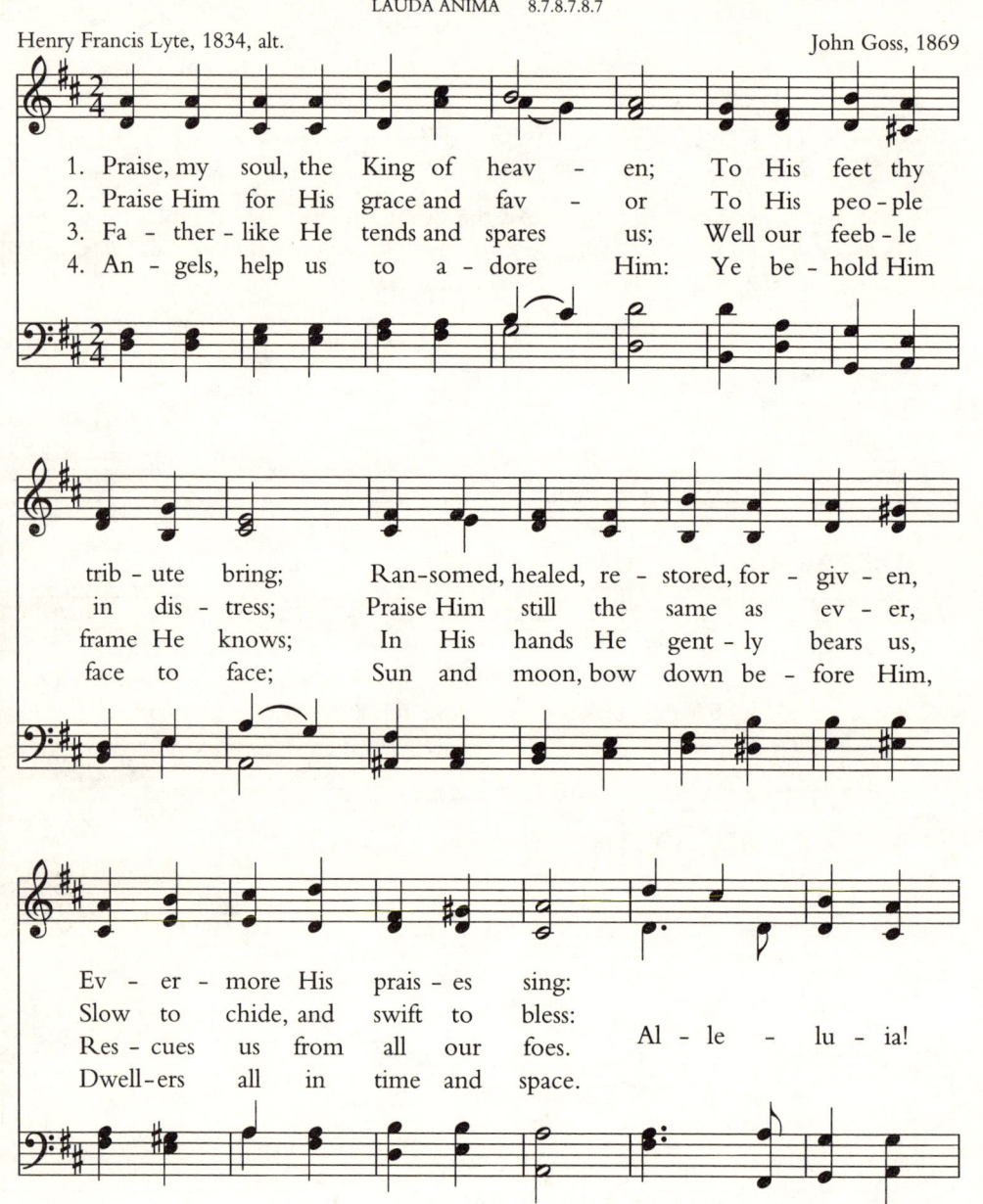

99 Praise, My Soul, the King of Heaven
LAUDA ANIMA 8.7.8.7.8.7

Henry Francis Lyte, 1834, alt.
John Goss, 1869

1. Praise, my soul, the King of heaven; To His feet thy
2. Praise Him for His grace and favor To His people
3. Father-like He tends and spares us; Well our feeble
4. Angels, help us to adore Him: Ye behold Him

tribute bring; Ransomed, healed, restored, forgiven,
in distress; Praise Him still the same as ever,
frame He knows; In His hands He gently bears us,
face to face; Sun and moon, bow down before Him,

Evermore His praises sing;
Slow to chide, and swift to bless:
Rescues us from all our foes. Alleluia!
Dwellers all in time and space.

Note: ♩ = 48–52

MORNING AND OPENING HYMNS

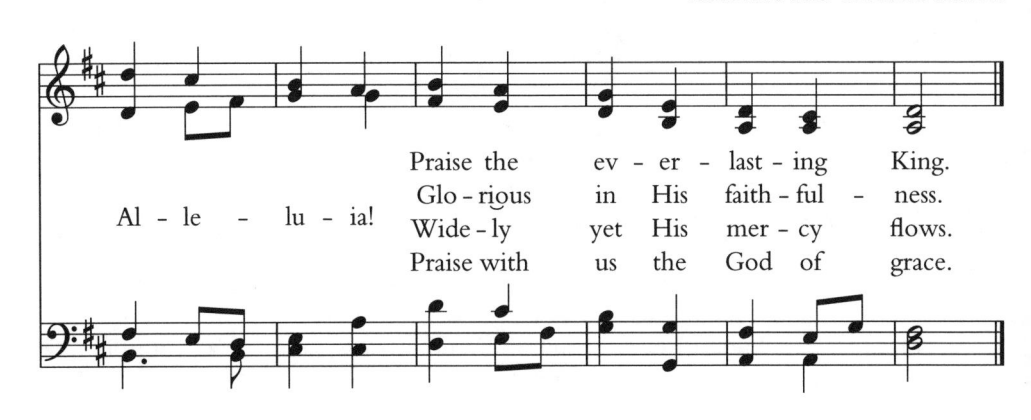

Al - le - lu - ia! Praise the ev - er - last - ing King.
Glo - rious in His faith - ful - ness.
Wide - ly yet His mer - cy flows.
Praise with us the God of grace.

Alternate harmony — John Goss, 1869

MORNING AND OPENING HYMNS

100 Ye Servants of God, Your Master Proclaim
HANOVER 10.10.11.11

Charles Wesley, 1744

attr. William Croft, 1708
A Supplement to the New Version of the Psalms, 1708

1. Ye servants of God, your Master proclaim,
And publish abroad His wonderful Name;
The Name all-victorious of Jesus extol;
His kingdom is glorious; He rules over all.

2. God ruleth on high, almighty to save;
And still He is nigh— His presence we have;
The great congregation His triumph shall sing,
Ascribing salvation to Jesus our King.

3. "Salvation to God, Who sits on the throne,"
Let all cry aloud and honor the Son;
The praises of Jesus the angels proclaim,
Fall down on their faces, and worship the Lamb.

4. Then let us adore and give Him His right,
All glory and power, all wisdom and might,
All honor and blessing, with angels above,
And thanks never ceasing, and infinite love.

MORNING AND OPENING HYMNS

When Morning Gilds the Skies

LAUDES DOMINI 6.6.6.D

101

German hymn, c. 1800
trans. Edward Caswall, 1853, 1858; alt.

Joseph Barnby, 1868

1. When morn-ing gilds the skies, My heart a-wak-ing cries:
2. Does sad-ness fill my mind? A sol-ace here I find:
3. Let earth's wide cir-cle round in joy-ful notes re-sound:
4. Be this while life is mine, My can-ti-cle div-ine:

A-like at work and prayer
Or fades my earth-ly bliss?
Let air and sea and sky
Be this the e-ter-nal song

May Je-sus Christ be praised!

To Je-sus I re-pair:
My com-fort still is this:
From depth to height re-ply:
Through all the a-ges long:

May Je-sus Christ be praised!

MORNING AND OPENING HYMNS

102 To God Be the Glory
TO GOD BE THE GLORY 11.11.11.11 with Refrain

Fanny Jane Crosby, 1875
William Howard Doane, 1875

1. To God be the glory, great things He hath done!
So loved He the world that He gave us His Son,
Who yielded His life an atonement for sin,
And opened the life-gate, that all may go in.

2. Great things He hath taught us, great things He hath done,
And great our rejoicing through Jesus the Son;
But purer and higher and greater will be
Our wonder, our transport, when Jesus we see.

MORNING AND OPENING HYMNS

Refrain

Praise the Lord, praise the Lord, Let the earth hear His voice!

Praise the Lord, praise the Lord, Let the people rejoice!

Oh, come to the Father through Jesus the Son,

And give Him the glory: great things He hath done!

SACRAMENTS

103 Let Us Break Bread Together
LET US BREAK BREAD 10.10 with Refrain

African-American spiritual

African-American spiritual
arr. Melva Wilson Costen, 1988

1. Let us break bread to-geth-er on our knees; (on our knees;)
2. Let us drink wine to-geth-er on our knees;

Let us break bread to-geth-er on our knees. (on our knees.)
Let us drink wine to-geth-er on our knees.

Refrain
When I fall on my knees with my face to the ris-ing sun,
O Lord, have mer-cy on me. (on me.)

Music: arrangement © 1990 Melva Wilson Costen. All rights reserved. Used by permission.

SACRAMENTS

3. Let us praise God together on our knees; *(on our knees;)*
(knees;)

Let us praise God together on our knees.

Refrain
When I fall on my knees with my face to the rising sun,
O Lord, have mercy on me. *(on me.)*

SACRAMENTS

104 There Is a Fountain Filled with Blood
CLEANSING FOUNTAIN   C.M.D

William Cowper, ca. 1771 (Zech. 13:1)   19th cent. USA camp meeting melody

1. There is a foun-tain filled with blood Drawn from Em-man-uel's veins; And sin-ners plunged be-neath that flood Lose all their guilt-y stains.
2. The dy-ing thief re-joiced to see That foun-tain in his day; And there may I, though vile as he, Wash all my sins a-way.
3. Dear dy-ing Lamb, Thy pre-cious blood Shall nev-er lose its power Till all the ran-somed church of God Be saved, to sin no more.
4. E'er since, by faith, I saw the stream Thy flow-ing wounds sup-ply, Re-deem-ing love has been my theme, And shall be till I die.
5. Then in a no-bler, sweet-er song, I'll sing Thy power to save, When this poor lisp-ing, stam-mering tongue Lies si-lent in the grave.

SACRAMENTS

Lose all their guilt-y stains, Lose all their guilt-y stains; And sin-ners plunged be-neath that flood Lose all their guilt-y stains.
Wash all my sins a - way, Wash all my sins a - way; And there may I, though vile as he, Wash all my sins a - way.
Be saved, to sin no more, Be saved, to sin no more; Till all the ran-somed church of God Be saved, to sin no more.
And shall be till I die, And shall be till I die; Re - deem-ing love has been my theme, And shall be till I die.
Lies si - lent in the grave, Lies si - lent in the grave; When this poor lisp-ing, stam-mering tongue Lies si - lent in the grave.

SACRAMENTS

105

Here, O Our Lord, We See You Face to Face

ADORO TE DEVOTE   10.10.10.10

Horatius Bonar, 1855; alt. 1972

Benedictine plainsong, Mode V, 13th century
as in *Hymnal for Colleges and Schools*, 1956

1. Here, O our Lord, we see You face to face.
2. We have no help but Yours, nor do we need
3. This is the hour of ban-quet and of song:
4. Too soon we rise; the sym-bols dis-ap-pear.
5. Feast aft-er feast thus comes and pass-es by,

Here would we touch and hand-le things un-seen.
An-oth-er arm save Yours to lean up-on.
This is the heaven-ly ta-ble for us spread;
The feast, though not the love, is past and gone;
Yet, pass-ing, points to that glad feast a-bove,

Music: harmonization © 1956 Yale University Press. All rights reserved. Used by permission.

SACRAMENTS

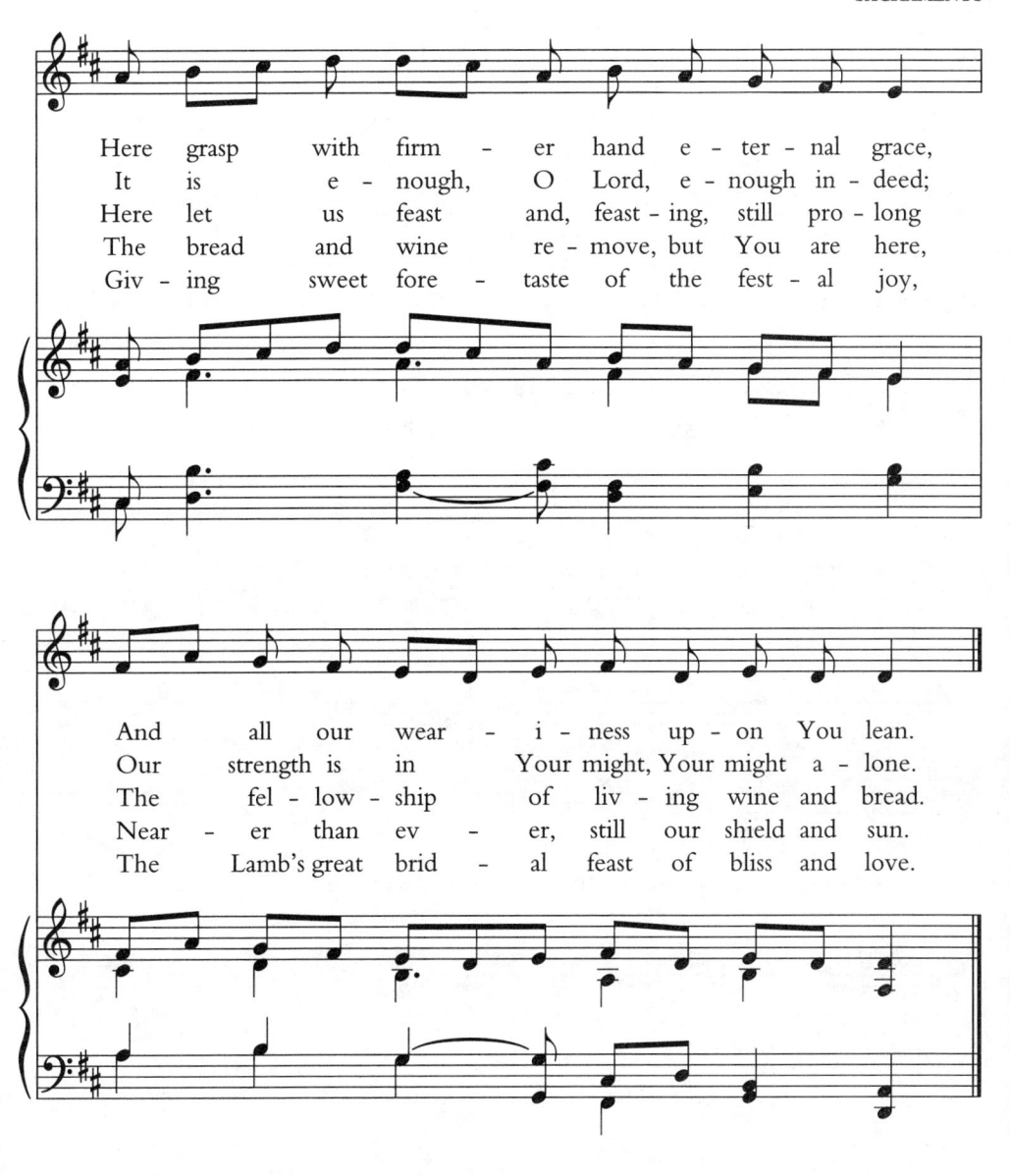

Here grasp with firmer hand eternal grace,
And all our weariness upon You lean.

It is enough, O Lord, enough indeed;
Our strength is in Your might, Your might alone.

Here let us feast and, feasting, still prolong
The fellowship of living wine and bread.

The bread and wine remove, but You are here,
Nearer than ever, still our shield and sun.

Giving sweet foretaste of the festal joy,
The Lamb's great bridal feast of bliss and love.

ORDINATION AND CONFIRMATION

106 Here I Am, Lord
HERE I AM, LORD 7.7.7.4.D with Refrain

Daniel L. Schutte, 1981, alt.

Daniel L. Schutte, 1981
harm. Michael Pope, Daniel L. Schutte, and John Weissrock, 1983

1. I, the Lord of sea and sky, I have heard My peo-ple cry.
2. I, the Lord of snow and rain, I have borne My peo-ple's pain.
3. I, the Lord of wind and flame, I will tend the poor and lame.

All who dwell in deep-est sin My hand will save.
I have wept for love of them. They turn a-way.
I will set a feast for them. My hand will save.

I Who made the stars of night, I will make their dark-ness bright.
I will break their hearts of stone, Give them hearts for love a-lone.
Fin-est bread I will pro-vide Till their hearts be sat-is-fied.

Words and Music: © 1981, Daniel L. Schutte and New Dawn Music, 5536 NE Hassalo, Portland, OR 97213. All rights reserved. Used with permission.

ORDINATION AND CONFIRMATION

Who will bear My light to them?
I will speak My word to them. Whom shall I send?
I will give My life to them.

Refrain—unison

Here I am, Lord, Is it I, Lord? I have heard You calling in the night. I will go, Lord, if You lead me. I will hold Your people in my heart.

Fine Interlude

FUNERAL

107 When the Trumpet of the Lord
When the Roll Is Called up Yonder
ROLL CALL   Irregular with Refrain

James M. Black (1856–1938)   James M. Black (1856–1938)

1. When the trum-pet of the Lord shall sound, and time shall be no more,
2. On that bright and cloud-less morn-ing when the dead in Christ shall rise,
3. Let us la - bor for the Mas - ter from the dawn till set - ting sun,

And the morn-ing breaks, e - ter - nal, bright, and fair; When the
And the glo - ry of His res - ur - rec - tion share; When His
Let us talk of all His won-drous love and care; Then when

saved of earth shall gath - er o - ver on the oth - er shore,
chos - en ones shall gath - er to their home be-yond the skies,
all of life is o - ver, and our work on earth is done,

And the roll is called up yon - der, I'll be there.

FUNERAL

FUNERAL

108 For All the Saints
SINE NOMINE   10.10.10 with Alleluias

William Walsham How, 1864   Ralph Vaughan Williams, 1906

1. For all the saints who from their la-bors rest, Who
2. Thou wast their rock, their for-tress, and their might;
*3. O blest com-mun - ion, fel-low-ship div - ine!
**4. From earth's wide bounds, from o-cean's far-thest coast, Through

Thee by faith be - fore the world con-fessed, Thy
Thou, Lord, their cap - tain in the well-fought fight;
We feeb-ly strug - gle, they in glo - ry shine; Yet
gates of pearl streams in the count-less host,

name, O Je - sus, be for-ev - er blest.
Thou, in the dark - ness drear, their one true light.
all are one in Thee, for all are Thine.
Sing - ing to Fa - ther, Son, and Ho - ly Ghost,

Music: from *The English Hymnal*, 1906. Used by permission of Oxford University Press.

FUNERAL

Harmony, stanza 3

3. O blest communion, fellowship divine! We feebly struggle, they in glory shine; Yet all are one in Thee, for all are Thine. Alleluia! Alleluia!

D.C. for stanza 4

★ *(May be sung before stanza 3)*

> Oh, may Thy soldiers, faithful, true, and bold,
> Fight as the saints who nobly fought of old,
> And win with them the victor's crown of gold.
> Alleluia! Alleluia!

★★ *(May be sung before stanza 4)*

> And when the strife is fierce, the warfare long,
> Steals on the ear the distant triumph song,
> And hearts are brave again, and arms are strong.
> Alleluia! Alleluia!

FUNERAL

109 Near to the Heart of God

McAFEE   C.M. with Refrain

Cleland Boyd McAfee, 1901 — Cleland Boyd McAfee, 1901

1. There is a place of quiet rest, Near to the heart of God,
A place where sin cannot molest, Near to the heart of God.

2. There is a place of comfort sweet, Near to the heart of God,
A place where we our Savior meet, Near to the heart of God.

3. There is a place of full release, Near to the heart of God,
A place where all is joy and peace, Near to the heart of God.

Refrain
O Jesus, blest Redeemer, Sent from the heart of God,
Hold us, who wait before Thee, Near to the heart of God.

FUNERAL

There's a Land That Is Fairer Than Day 110
Sweet By and By
SWEET BY AND BY   9.9.9.9 with Refrain

Sanford F. Bennett (1836–1898)　　　　　　　　　　　Joseph P. Webster (1819–1875)

1. There's a land that is fair-er than day, And by faith we can see it a-far: For the Fa-ther waits o-ver the way To pre-pare us a dwell-ing-place there.
2. We shall sing on that beau-ti-ful shore The mel-o-di-ous songs of the blest, And our spir-its shall sor-row no more, Not a sigh for the bless-ing of rest.
3. To our boun-ti-ful Fa-ther a-bove We will of-fer the trib-ute of praise For the glo-ri-ous gift of His love And the bless-ings that hal-low our days.

Refrain
In the sweet by and by, (*In the sweet*) (*by and by,*) We shall meet on that beau-ti-ful shore; (*by and by;*) In the sweet by and by, (*In the sweet*) (*by and by,*) We shall meet on that beau-ti-ful shore.

FUNERAL

111 Swing Low, Sweet Chariot
SWING LOW 10.8.10.8 with Refrain

African-American spiritual (2 Kg. 2:11)

African-American spiritual
adapt. and arr. by William Farley Smith, 1987

Refrain

Swing low, sweet chariot, Coming for to carry me home; Swing low, sweet chariot, Coming for to carry me home. *Fine*

1. I looked o-ver Jor-dan, and what did I see,
2. If you get there be-fore I do,
3. I'm some-times up, I'm some-times down,
4. The bright-est day that I can say,

Music: adaptation and arrangement © 1989 The United Methodist Publishing House (Administered by The Copyright Company c/o The Copyright Company, Nashville, TN). All rights reserved. International copyright secured. Used by permission.

FUNERAL

Com-ing for to car-ry me home;
A band of an-gels com-ing af-ter me,
Tell all my friends I'm com-ing too,
But still my soul feels heav-en-ly bound,
When Je-sus washed my sins a-way,
Com-ing for to car-ry me home.

D.C.

EVENING HYMNS

112 — Abide with Me
EVENTIDE   10.10.10.10

Henry Francis Lyte, 1847 — William Henry Monk, 1861

1. A-bide with me: fast falls the e-ven-tide;
The dark-ness deep-ens; Lord, with me a-bide!
When oth-er help-ers fail and com-forts flee,
Help of the help-less, oh, a-bide with me.

2. Swift to its close ebbs out life's lit-tle day;
Earth's joys grow dim, its glo-ries pass a-way;
Change and de-cay in all a-round I see.
O Thou who chang-est not, a-bide with me.

3. I need Thy pres-ence ev-ery pass-ing hour;
What but Thy grace can foil the tempt-er's power?
Who, like Thy-self, my guide and stay can be?
Through cloud and sun-shine, Lord, a-bide with me.

4. I fear no foe with Thee at hand to bless:
Ills have no weight, and tears no bit-ter-ness.
Where is death's sting? Where, grave, Thy vic-to-ry?
I tri-umph still, if Thou a-bide with me.

5. Hold Thou Thy cross before my closing eyes;
Shine through the gloom and point me to the skies;
Heaven's morning breaks, and earth's vain shadows flee;
In life, in death, O Lord, abide with me.

EVENING HYMNS

Out of My Bondage, Sorrow, and Night 113

William T. Sleeper (1819–1904) George C. Stebbins (1846–1945)

1. Out of my bond-age, sor-row, and night, Je-sus, I come, Je-sus, I come;
2. Out of my shame-ful fail-ure and loss,
3. Out of the fear and dread of the tomb,

In - to Your free-dom, glad-ness, and light,
In - to the glo-rious gain of Your cross, Je-sus, I come to you.
In - to the joy and light of Your home,

Out of my sick-ness in - to Your health, Out of my want and in - to Your
Out of earth's sor-rows in - to Your balm, Out of life's storms and in - to Your
Out of the depths of ru - in un - told, In-to the peace of Your shel-ter-ing

wealth, Out of my sin and in - to Your-self,
calm, Out of dis-tress to ju - bi-lant psalm, Je-sus, I come to you.
fold, Ev - er Your glo-rious face to be - hold,

ANY OCCASION

114 Hiding in Thee

William O. Cushing (1823–1902)
Ira D. Sankey (1840–1908)

1. O__ safe to the Rock that is high-er than I,
2. In the calm of the noon-tide, in sor-row's lone hour,
3. How oft in the con-flict, when pressed by the foe,

My__ soul in its con-flicts and sor-rows would fly;
In__ times when temp-ta-tion casts o'er me its power;
I have fled to my Ref-uge and breathed out my woe;

So__ sin-ful, so wea-ry, Thine, Thine would I be;
In the tem-pests of life, on its wide, heav-ing sea,
How oft-en, when tri-als like sea-bil-lows roll,

ANY OCCASION

Thou blest "Rock of A - ges," I'm hid - ing in Thee.
Thou blest "Rock of A - ges," I'm hid - ing in Thee.
Have I hid - den in Thee, O Thou Rock of my soul.

Refrain
Hid - ing in Thee, hid - ing in Thee, Thou blest "Rock of A - ges," I'm hid - ing in Thee.

ANY OCCASION

115 Yield Not to Temptation

Horatio R. Palmer (1834–1907)   Horatio R. Palmer (1834–1907)

1. Yield not to temp-ta-tion, For yield-ing is sin. Each vic-t'ry will help you Some oth-er to win. Fight man-ful-ly on-ward, Dark pas-sions sub-due.
2. Shun e-vil com-pan-ions, Bad lan-guage dis-dain. God's name hold in rev-'rence, Nor take it in vain; Be thought-ful and ear-nest, Kind-heart-ed and true. Look ev-er to Je-sus; He will car-ry you through.
3. To him that o'er-com-eth God giv-eth a crown; Through faith we shall con-quer, Though oft-en cast down; He Who is our Sav-ior Our strength will re-new.

Refrain

Ask the Sav-ior to help you, Com-fort, strength-en, and keep you.
He is will-ing to aid you; He will car-ry you through.

Music: arr. copyright, © 1957, by Hope Publishing Co. International copyright secured. All rights reserved.

ANY OCCASION

The Great Physician

GREAT PHYSICIAN 8.7.8.7 with Refrain

116

William Hunter (1811–1877)   John H. Stockton (1813–1877)

1. The great Physician now is near, The sympathizing Jesus;
2. Your many sins are all forgiven; Oh! hear the voice of Jesus;
3. All glory to the dying Lamb! I now believe in Jesus;
4. His name dispels my guilt and fear, No other name but Jesus;

He speaks the drooping heart to cheer, Oh! Hear the voice of Jesus.
Go on your way in peace to heaven And wear a crown with Jesus.
I love the blessed Savior's name, I love the name of Jesus.
Oh! how my soul delights to hear The charming name of Jesus.

Refrain

Sweetest note in seraph song, Sweetest name on mortal tongue;
Sweetest carol ever sung, Jesus, blessed Jesus.

ANY OCCASION

117 True-Hearted, Whole-Hearted

Frances R. Havergal (1836–1879)   George C. Stebbins (1846–1945)

1. faith - ful and loy - al,
2. True - heart - ed, whole - heart - ed, full - est al - le - giance
3. Sav - ior all - glo - rious!

King of our lives, by Thy grace we will be;
Yield - ing hence-forth to our glo - ri - ous King;
Take Thy great pow - er and reign there a - lone,

Un - der the stand - ard ex - alt - ed and roy - al,
Val - iant en - deav - or and lov - ing o - be - dience,
O - ver our wills and af - fec - tions vic - to - rious,

Strong in Thy strength we will bat - tle for Thee.
Free - ly and joy - ous - ly now would we bring.
Free - ly sur - ren - dered and whol - ly Thine own.

ANY OCCASION

Refrain

Peal out the watch-word! silence it never!
Song of our spirits, rejoicing and free;
Peal out the watch-word! loyal forever,
King of our lives, by Thy grace we will be.

ANY OCCASION

118 Send the Light

McCABE Irregular

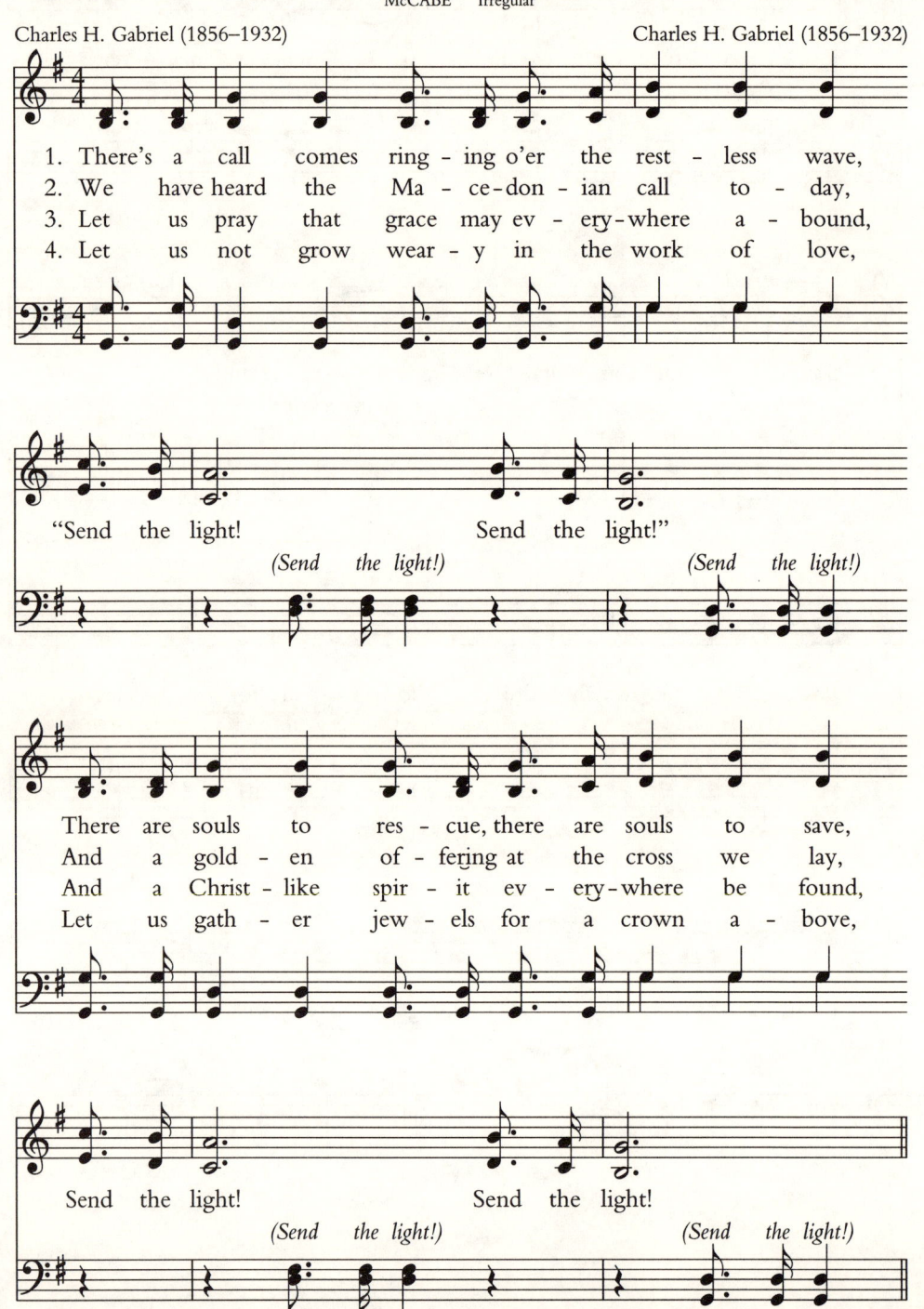

Charles H. Gabriel (1856–1932) Charles H. Gabriel (1856–1932)

1. There's a call comes ringing o'er the restless wave,
2. We have heard the Macedonian call today,
3. Let us pray that grace may everywhere abound,
4. Let us not grow weary in the work of love,

"Send the light! Send the light!"
(Send the light!) *(Send the light!)*

There are souls to rescue, there are souls to save,
And a golden offering at the cross we lay,
And a Christ-like spirit everywhere be found,
Let us gather jewels for a crown above,

Send the light! Send the light!
(Send the light!) *(Send the light!)*

ANY OCCASION

ANY OCCASION

119 Redeemed, How I Love to Proclaim It

REDEEMED 9.8.9.8 with Refrain

Fanny J. Crosby (1820–1915) William J. Kirkpatrick (1838–1921)

1. Redeemed, how I love to proclaim it!
2. Redeemed, and so happy in Jesus,
3. I think of my blessed Redeemer,
4. I know I shall see in His beauty

Redeemed by the blood of the Lamb;
No language my rapture can tell;
I think of Him all the day long;
The King in Whose law I delight;

Redeemed through His infinite mercy,
I know that the light of His presence
I sing, for I cannot be silent;
Who lovingly guardeth my footsteps

His child, and forever, I am.
With me doth continually dwell.
His love is the theme of my song.
And giveth me songs in the night.

ANY OCCASION

Refrain

Re - deemed, re - deemed, Re - deemed by the
(Re - deemed,) *(re - deemed,)*

blood of the Lamb; Re - deemed, re -
(Re - deemed,)

deemed, His child, and for - ev - er, I am.
(re - deemed,)

ANY OCCASION

120 Count Your Blessings

BLESSINGS 11.11.11.11 with Refrain

Johnson Oatman, Jr. (1856–1922) Edwin O. Excell (1851–1921)

1. When up-on life's bil-lows you are tem-pest-tossed,
2. Are you ev-er bur-dened with a load of care?
3. When you look at oth-ers with their lands and gold,
4. So, a-mid the con-flict, wheth-er great or small,

When you are dis-cour-aged, think-ing all is lost,
Does the cross seem heav-y you are called to bear?
Think that Christ has prom-ised you His wealth un-told;
Do not be dis-cour-aged, God is o-ver all;

Count your man-y bless-ings,
    name them one by one,
    ev-ery doubt will fly,
    mon-ey can-not buy
    an-gels will at-tend,

And it will sur-prise you what the Lord hath done.
And you will be sing-ing as the days go by.
Your re-ward in heav-en, nor your home on high.
Help and com-fort give you to your jour-ney's end.

ANY OCCASION

Refrain

Count your bless-ings, name them one by one;
(Count your man-y bless-ings,) *(name them one by one;)*

Count your bless-ings, see what God hath done;
(Count your man-y bless-ings,) *(see what God hath done;)*

Count your bless-ings, name them one by one;
(Count your man-y bless-ings,)

Count your man-y bless-ings, see what God hath done.

ANY OCCASION

121 Faith Is the Victory

SANKEY C.M.D with Refrain

John H. Yates (1837–1900) Ira D. Sankey (1840–1908)

1. En-camped a-long the hills of light, Ye Chris-tian sol-diers, rise, And press the bat-tle ere the night Shall veil the glow-ing skies. A-gainst the foe in vales be-low Let all our strength be hurled; Faith is the
2. His ban-ner o-ver us is love, Our sword the Word of God; We tread the road the saints a-bove With shouts of tri-umph trod. By faith they, like a whirl-wind's breath, Swept on o'er ev-ery field; The faith by
3. To him who o-ver-comes the foe White rai-ment shall be given; Be-fore the an-gels he shall know His name con-fessed in heaven. Then on-ward from the hills of light, Our hearts with love a-flame; We'll van-quish

ANY OCCASION

vic - to - ry, we know, That o - ver-comes the world.
which they con - quered death Is still our shin - ing shield.
all the hosts of night In Je - sus' con - quering name.

Refrain

Faith __ is the vic - to - ry! Faith __ is the vic - to - ry!
(Faith)   (Faith)

Oh, glo - ri - ous vic - to - ry that o - ver-comes the world.

ANY OCCASION

122 Sunshine in My Soul
SUNSHINE   Irregular

Eliza E. Hewitt (1851–1920)   John R. Sweney (1837–1899)

1. sunshine in my soul to-day, More glorious and bright
2. music in my soul to-day, A carol to my King;
3. There is music in my soul to-day, For when my Lord is near,
4. gladness in my soul to-day, And hope and praise and love

Than glows in any earthly sky, For Jesus is my light.
And Jesus, listening, can hear The songs I cannot sing.
The dove of peace sings in my heart, The flowers of grace appear.
For blessings which He gives me now, For joys "laid up" above.

Oh, there's sunshine, blessed sunshine,
(sunshine in my soul,)   (sunshine in my soul,)

When the peaceful, happy moments roll;   When
(happy moments roll;)

ANY OCCASION

Je-sus shows His smil-ing face, There is sun-shine in my soul.

Praise Him, All Ye Little Children 123
BONNER 10.6.10.6

Anonymous Carey Bonner (1859–1938)

1. Praise Him, praise Him,
2. Love Him, love Him, All ye lit-tle chil-dren, God is love, God is love;
3. Thank Him, thank Him,

Praise Him, praise Him,
Love Him, love Him, All ye lit-tle chil-dren, God is love, God is love.
Thank Him, thank Him,

ANY OCCASION

124 Steal Away to Jesus

STEAL AWAY 5.7.8.7 with Refrain

African-American spiritual (1 Cor. 15:51–52)

African-American spiritual
adapt. and arr. by William Farley Smith, 1986

Refrain

Steal a-way, steal a-way; Steal a-way to Je-sus.
Steal a-way, steal a-way home. I ain't got long to stay here.

Fine

1. My Lord, he calls me, He calls me by the thun-der;
2. Green trees a-bend-ing, Poor sin-ners stand a trem-bling; The
3. My Lord, he calls me, He calls me by the light-ning;

trum-pet sounds with-in-a my soul. I ain't got long to stay here.

D.C.

Music: © 1989 The United Methodist Publishing House (Administered by The Copyright Company c/o The Copyright Company, Nashville, TN). All rights reserved. International copyright secured. Used by permission.

ANY OCCASION

There Shall Be Showers of Blessing 125

SHOWERS OF BLESSING 8.7.8.7. with Refrain

Daniel W. Whittle (1840–1901); alt. (Ez. 34:26) James McGranahan (1840–1907)

1. There shall be show-ers of bless-ing: This is the prom-ise of love;
2. There shall be show-ers of bless-ing: Pre-cious re-viv-ing a-gain;
3. There shall be show-ers of bless-ing: Send them up-on us, O Lord;
4. There shall be show-ers of bless-ing: Oh, that to-day they might fall,

There shall be sea-sons re-fresh-ing, Sent from the Sav-ior a-bove.
O-ver the hills and the val-leys, Sound of a-bun-dance of rain.
Grant to us now a re-fresh-ing, Come and now hon-or Your Word.
Now as to God we're con-fess-ing, Now as on Je-sus we call!

Refrain

Show - ers of bless - ing, Show-ers of bless-ing we need:
(Show - ers, show-ers)

Mer-cy-drops 'round us are fall - ing, But for the show-ers we plead.

ANY OCCASION

126 Precious Name
PRECIOUS NAME 8.7.8.7 with Refrain

Lydia Baxter, 1870 (Phil. 2:9–11)
William H. Doane, 1871

1. Take the name of Jesus with you, Child of sorrow and of woe; It will joy and comfort give you; Take it then, wher-e'er you go.
2. Take the name of Jesus ever As a shield from every snare; If temptations 'round you gather, Breathe that holy name in prayer.
3. Oh, the precious name of Jesus! How it thrills our souls with joy, When His loving arms receive us, And His songs our tongues employ!
4. At the name of Jesus bowing, Falling prostrate at His feet, King of kings in heaven we'll crown Him, When our journey is complete.

ANY OCCASION

Refrain

Precious name, Oh, how sweet!
(Precious name,) *(Oh, how sweet!)*
Hope of earth and joy of heaven. Precious name,
(Precious name,)
Oh, how sweet! Hope of earth and joy of heaven.
(how sweet!)

ANY OCCASION

127 Give Me Jesus

Traditional
Traditional
harm. by Verolga Nix, b. 1933

Slowly

1. I heard my moth-er say, I heard my moth-er say,
2. Dark mid-night was my cry, Dark mid-night was my cry,
3. Oh, when I come to die, Oh, when I come to die,

I heard my moth-er say,
Dark mid-night was my cry, Give me Je - sus.
Oh, when I come to die,

Refrain

Give me Je - sus, Give me Je - sus,

You may have all this world, Give me Je - sus.

Music: harm. copyright © 1981 by Abingdon.

ANY OCCASION

Take Time to Be Holy

128

HOLINESS 6.5.6.5.D

William D. Longstaff, ca. 1882 (1 Pet. 1:16) — George C. Stebbins, 1890

1. Take time to be holy, speak oft with thy Lord;
Abide in Him always, and feed on His word.
Make friends of God's children, help those who are weak,
Forgetting in nothing His blessing to seek.

2. Take time to be holy, the world rushes on;
Spend much time in secret with Jesus alone.
By looking to Jesus, like Him thou shalt be;
Thy friends in thy conduct His likeness shall see.

3. Take time to be holy, let Him be thy guide,
And run not before Him, whatever betide.
In joy or in sorrow, still follow the Lord,
And, looking to Jesus, still trust in His word.

4. Take time to be holy, be calm in thy soul,
Each thought and each motive beneath His control.
Thus led by His Spirit to fountains of love,
Thou soon shalt be fitted for service above.

ANY OCCASION

129 'Tis So Sweet to Trust in Jesus

TRUST IN JESUS 8.7.8.7 with Refrain

Louisa M. R. Stead, 1882
William J. Kirkpatrick, 1882

1. 'Tis so sweet to trust in Je-sus And to take Him at His word; Just to rest up-on His prom-ise, And to know, "Thus saith the Lord."
2. Oh, how sweet to trust in Je-sus, Just to trust His cleans-ing blood; And in sim-ple faith to plunge me 'Neath the heal-ing, cleans-ing flood!
3. Yes, 'tis sweet to trust in Je-sus, Just from sin and self to cease; Just from Je-sus simp-ly tak-ing Life and rest, and joy and peace.
4. I'm so glad I learned to trust Thee, Pre-cious Je-sus, Sav-ior, Friend; And I know that Thou art with me, Wilt be with me to the end.

Refrain

Je-sus, Je-sus, how I trust Him! How I've proved Him o'er and o'er! Je-sus, Je-sus,

ANY OCCASION

pre - cious Je - sus! Oh, for grace to trust Him more!

Lord, Speak to Me   130
CANONBURY   L.M.

Frances R. Havergal, 1872 (Rom. 14:7)   adapt. from Robert Schumann, 1839

1. Lord, speak to me, that I may speak In
2. Oh, strength-en me, that while I stand Firm
3. Oh, teach me, Lord, that I may teach The
4. Oh, fill me with Thy full - ness, Lord, Un -
5. Oh, use me, Lord, use e - ven me, Just

liv - ing ech - oes of Thy tone; As Thou hast sought, so
on the rock, and strong in Thee, I may stretch out a
pre - cious things Thou dost im - part; And wing my words, that
til my ver - y heart o'er - flow In kind - ling thought and
as Thou wilt, and when, and where, Un - til Thy bless - ed

let me seek Thine err - ing chil - dren lost and lone.
lov - ing hand To wrest - lers with the trou - bled sea.
they may reach The hid - den depths of man - y a heart.
glow - ing word, Thy love to tell, Thy praise to show.
face I see, Thy rest, Thy joy, Thy glo - ry share.

ANY OCCASION

131 I Surrender All

SURRENDER 8.7.8.7 with Refrain

J.W. Van Deventer, 1896   W.S. Weeden, 1896

1. All to Him I freely give; I will ever love and trust Him, In His presence daily live.
2. Humbly at His feet I bow, Worldly pleasures all forsaken; Take me, Jesus, take me now.
3. All to Jesus I surrender; Make me, Savior, wholly Thine; Let me feel the Holy Spirit, Truly know that Thou art mine.
4. Lord, I give myself to Thee; Fill me with Thy love and power; Let Thy blessing fall on me.
5. Now I feel the sacred flame. Oh, the joy of full salvation! Glory, glory to His name!

Refrain (Harmony)

I surrender

ANY OCCASION

all,   I   sur-ren-der   all,
(I sur-ren-der all,)   *(I sur-ren-der all,)*

All   to Thee, my   bless-ed Sav-ior,   I   sur-ren-der   all.

ANY OCCASION

132 Are Ye Able
BEACON HILL Irregular

Earl Marlatt, 1926 (Mk. 10:35–40)　　　　　　　　　　　　　　Harry S. Mason, 1924

1. "Are ye a-ble," said the Mas-ter, "To be cru-ci-fied with Me?" "Yea," the stur-dy dream-ers ans-wered, "To the death we fol-low Thee."
2. Are ye a-ble to re-mem-ber, When a thief lifts up his eyes, That his par-doned soul is wor-thy Of a place in par-a-dise?
3. Are ye a-ble when the shad-ows Close a-round you with the sod, To be-lieve that spir-it tri-umphs, To com-mend your soul to God?
4. Are ye a-ble? Still the Mas-ter Whis-pers down e-ter-ni-ty, And he-ro-ic spir-its ans-wer, Now as then in Gal-i-lee.

ANY OCCASION

Refrain

Lord, we are able. Our spirits are Thine.
Re-mold them, make us, like Thee, divine.
Thy guiding radiance above us shall be
A beacon to God, to love, and loyalty.

ANY OCCASION

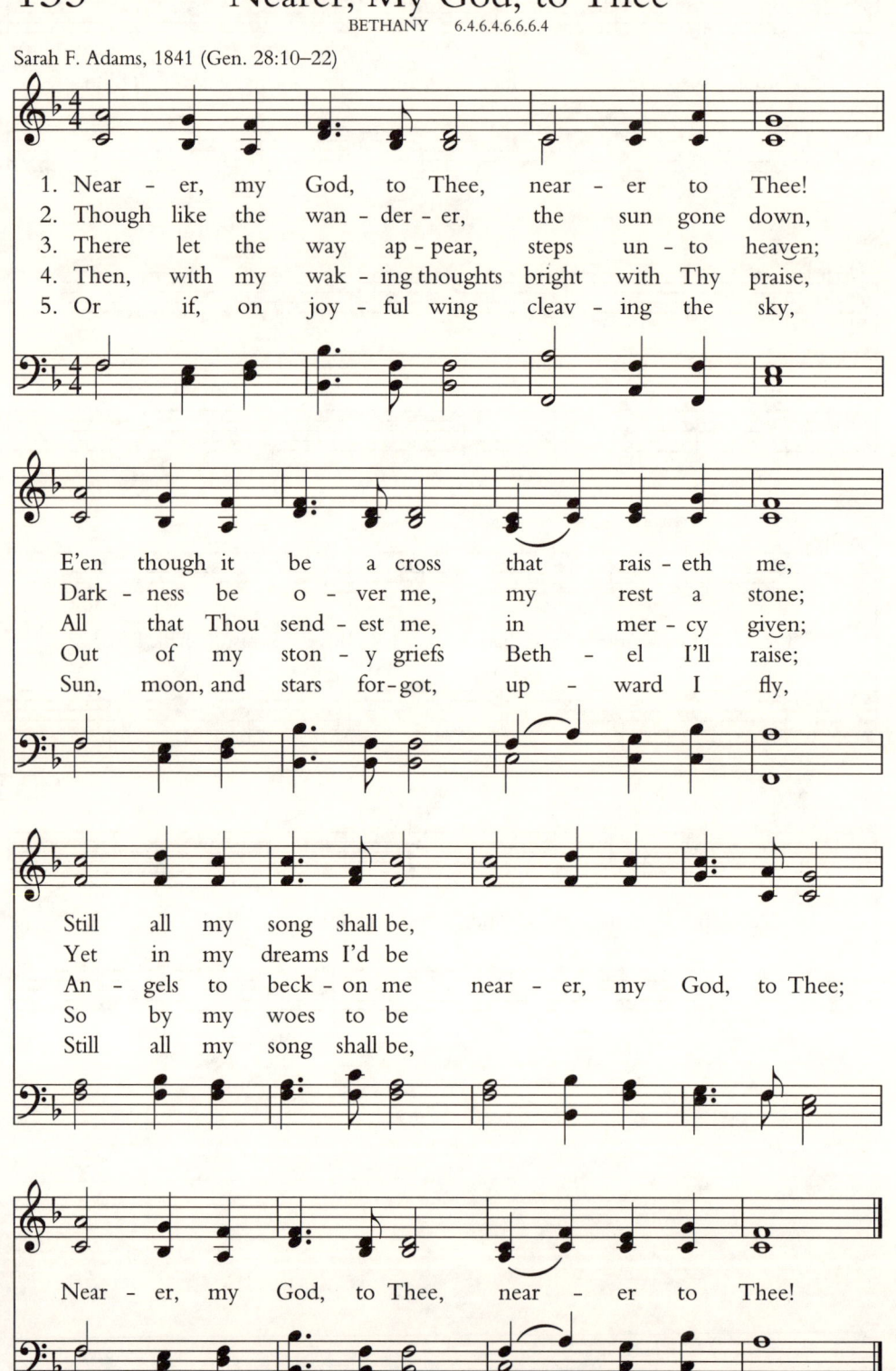

133 Nearer, My God, to Thee
BETHANY 6.4.6.4.6.6.6.4

Sarah F. Adams, 1841 (Gen. 28:10–22)

1. Near-er, my God, to Thee, near-er to Thee!
2. Though like the wan-der-er, the sun gone down,
3. There let the way ap-pear, steps un-to heaven;
4. Then, with my wak-ing thoughts bright with Thy praise,
5. Or if, on joy-ful wing cleav-ing the sky,

E'en though it be a cross that rais-eth me,
Dark-ness be o-ver me, my rest a stone;
All that Thou send-est me, in mer-cy given;
Out of my ston-y griefs Beth-el I'll raise;
Sun, moon, and stars for-got, up-ward I fly,

Still all my song shall be,
Yet in my dreams I'd be
An-gels to beck-on me nearer, my God, to Thee;
So by my woes to be
Still all my song shall be,

Near-er, my God, to Thee, near-er to Thee!

ANY OCCASION

I've Wandered Far Away from God 134

"Lord, I'm Coming Home"   8.5.8.5 with Refrain

William J. Kirkpatrick (1838–1921)   William J. Kirkpatrick (1838–1921)

1. I've wandered far away from God, The paths of sin too long I've trod, Now I'm coming home;
2. I've wasted many precious years, I now repent with bitter tears, Now I'm coming home;
3. I've tired of sin and straying, Lord, I'll trust Thy love, believe Thy word, Lord I'm coming home.
4. My soul is sick, my heart is sore, My strength renew, my hope restore,

Refrain

Coming home, coming home, Nevermore to roam, Open wide Thine arms of love, Lord, I'm coming home.

ANY OCCASION

135 Brightly Beams Our Father's Mercy
Let the Lower Lights Be Burning
LOWER LIGHTS   8.7.8.7 with Refrain

Philip P. Bliss (1838–1876)   Philip P. Bliss (1838–1876)

1. Bright-ly beams our Fa-ther's mer-cy From His light-house ev-er-more; But to us He gives the keep-ing Of the lights a-long the shore.
2. Dark the night of sin has set-tled, Loud the an-gry bil-lows roar; Ea-ger eyes are watch-ing, long-ing, For the lights a-long the shore.
3. Trim your fee-ble lamp, my broth-er! Some poor sea-man, tem-pest-tossed, Try-ing now to make the har-bor, In the dark-ness may be lost.

Refrain
Let the low-er lights be burn-ing! Send a gleam a-cross the wave! Some poor faint-ing, strug-gling sea-man You may res-cue, you may save.

ANY OCCASION

I Hear the Savior Say

Jesus Paid It All

ALL TO CHRIST   6.6.7.7 with Refrain

136

Elvina M. Hall (1820–1889)   John T. Grape (1835–1915)

1. I hear the Savior say, "Thy strength indeed is small,
Child of weakness, watch and pray, Find in Me thine all in all."

2. Lord, now indeed I find Thy power, and Thine alone
Can change the leper's spots And melt the heart of stone.

3. For nothing good have I Whereby Thy grace to claim;
I'll wash my garments white In the blood of Calvary's Lamb.

4. And when before the throne I stand in Him complete,
"Jesus died my soul to save," My lips shall still repeat.

Refrain

Jesus paid it all, All to Him I owe;
Sin had left a crimson stain; He washed it white as snow.

ANY OCCASION

137 I Was Sinking Deep in Sin
Love Lifted Me
SAFETY   Irregular with Refrain

James Rowe (1865–1933)   Howard E. Smith (1863–1918)

1. I was sinking deep in sin, Far from the peaceful shore,
Very deeply stained within, Sinking to rise no more;
But the Master of the sea Heard my despairing cry,

2. All my heart to Him I give, Ever to Him I'll cling,
In His blessed presence live, Ever His praises sing;
Love so mighty and so true Merits my soul's best songs;

3. Souls in danger, look above, Jesus completely saves;
He will lift you by His love Out of the angry waves;
He's the Master of the sea, Billows His will obey;

Words and music: copyright © 1911. Renewal 1939 by John T. Benson, Jr. Assigned to Singspiration, Division of Zondervan Corporation. All rights reserved. Used by permission.

ANY OCCASION

From the wa-ters lift-ed me, Now safe am I.
Faith-ful, lov-ing ser-vice, too, To Him be-longs.
He your Sav-ior wants to be, Be saved to-day.

Refrain
Love lift-ed me! Love lift-ed me! When noth-ing
(e - ven me!) *(e - ven me!)*
else could help, Love lift-ed me. Love lift-ed me.

ANY OCCASION

138 Pass Me Not, O Gentle Savior
PASS ME NOT 8.5.8.5 with Refrain

Fanny J. Crosby (1820–1915)
William H. Doane (1832–1915)

1. Pass me not, O gentle Savior, Hear my humble cry;
2. Let me at Thy throne of mercy Find a sweet relief;
3. Trusting only in Thy merit, Would I seek Thy face;
4. Thou the spring of all my comfort, More than life for me;

While on others Thou art calling, Do not pass me by.
Kneeling there in deep contrition, Help my unbelief.
Heal my wounded, broken spirit, Save me by Thy grace.
Whom have I on earth beside Thee? Whom in heaven but Thee?

Refrain

Savior, Savior, hear my humble cry, While on others Thou art calling, Do not pass me by. A-men.

ANY OCCASION

I Would Be True

139

PEEK 11.10.11.10.10

st. 1, 2, Howard Arnold Walter, 1917
st. 3, Anon., alt.

Joseph Y. Peek, 1911

1. I would be true, for there are those who trust me; I would be pure, for there are those who care; I would be strong, for there is much to suf-fer; I would be brave, for there is much to dare, I would be brave, for there is much to dare.

2. I would be friend of all, the foe, the friend-less; I would be giv-ing, and for-get the gift; I would be hum-ble, for I know my weak-ness; I would look up, and laugh, and love, and live, I would look up, and laugh, and love, and live.

3. I would be prayer-ful through each bus-y mo-ment; I would be con-stant-ly in touch with God; I would be tuned to sense God's slight-est whis-per; I would have faith to keep the path Christ trod, I would have faith to keep the path Christ trod.

Note: The first two stanzas of this hymn are from "My Creed," a poem that Howard Walter sent to his mother from Japan, where he taught English before becoming a Congregational minister. Walter died at the age of thirty-five while working for the Y.M.C.A. in India.

ANY OCCASION

140 My Soul in Sad Exile
The Haven of Rest
HAVEN OF REST Irregular with Refrain

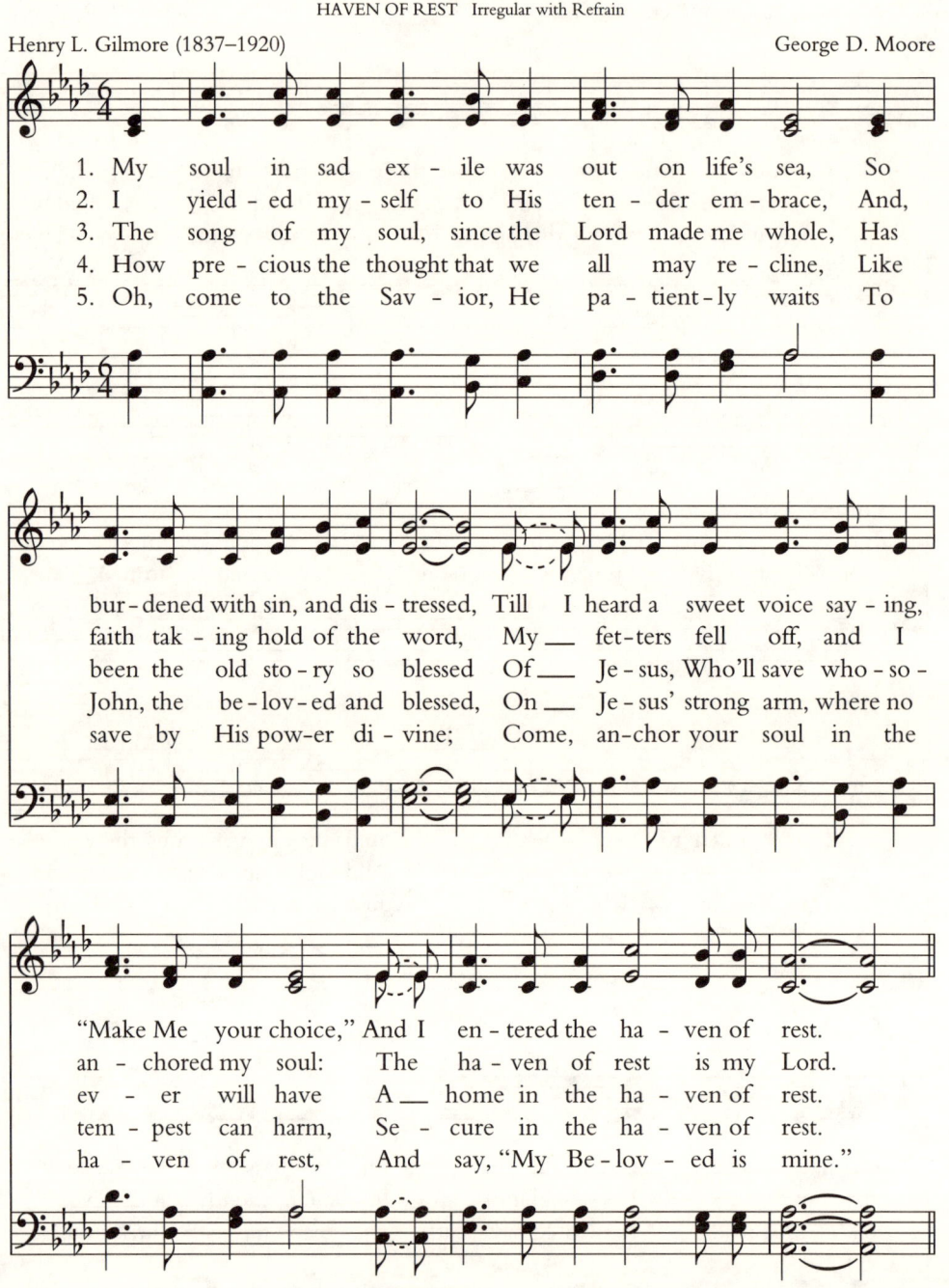

Henry L. Gilmore (1837–1920)　　　　　　　　　　　　　　　　George D. Moore

1. My soul in sad exile was out on life's sea, So burdened with sin, and distressed, Till I heard a sweet voice saying, "Make Me your choice," And I entered the haven of rest.
2. I yielded myself to His tender embrace, And, faith taking hold of the word, My fetters fell off, and I anchored my soul: The haven of rest is my Lord.
3. The song of my soul, since the Lord made me whole, Has been the old story so blessed Of Jesus, Who'll save whosoever will have A home in the haven of rest.
4. How precious the thought that we all may recline, Like John, the beloved and blessed, On Jesus' strong arm, where no tempest can harm, Secure in the haven of rest.
5. Oh, come to the Savior, He patiently waits To save by His power divine; Come, anchor your soul in the haven of rest, And say, "My Beloved is mine."

ANY OCCASION

Refrain

I've an-chored my soul in the ha-ven of rest, I'll sail the wide seas no more. The tem-pest may sweep o'er the wild storm-y deep; In Je-sus I'm safe ev-er-more.

ANY OCCASION

141 Sowing in the Morning
Bringing in the Sheaves
SHEAVES 12.11.12 1.11 with Refrain

Knowles Shaw (1834–1878)   George A. Minor

1. Sow-ing in the morn-ing, sow-ing seeds of kind-ness, Sow-ing in the noon-tide and the dew-y eve; Wait-ing for the har-vest and the time of reap-ing, We shall come re-joic-ing, bring-ing in the sheaves.

2. Sow-ing in the sun-shine, sow-ing in the shad-ows, Fear-ing neither clouds nor win-ter's chill-ing breeze; By and by the har-vest and the la-bor end-ed, We shall come re-joic-ing, bring-ing in the sheaves.

3. Go-ing forth with weep-ing, sow-ing for the Mas-ter, Though the loss sus-tained our spir-it oft-en grieves; When our weep-ing's o-ver He will bid us wel-come; We shall come re-joic-ing, bring-ing in the sheaves.

ANY OCCASION

Refrain

Bring-ing in the sheaves, Bring-ing in the sheaves, We shall come re-joic-ing, bring-ing in the sheaves; ing, bring-ing in the sheaves.

ANY OCCASION

142 I'm Pressing on the Upward Way
Higher Ground
HIGHER GROUND L.M. with Refrain

Johnson Oatman, Jr., 1892; alt. Charles H. Gabriel, 1898

1. I'm pressing on the upward way, New heights I'm gaining every day; Still praying as I'm onward bound, "O plant me, God, on higher ground."
2. My heart has no desire to stay Where doubts arise and fears dismay; Though some may dwell where these abound, My prayer, my aim is higher ground.
3. I want to live beyond the world, Though Satan's darts at me are hurled; For faith has caught a joyful sound, The song of saints on higher ground.
4. I want to scale the utmost height, And catch a gleam of glory bright; But still I'll pray till heaven I've found, "God, lead me on to higher ground."

Note: Johnson Oatman, Jr., wrote hymns while in the insurance business in Mount Holly, New Jersey. Words for more than 5,000 gospel songs are credited to him. Iowa-born Charles Gabriel taught singing schools and compiled many collections of gospel and Sunday School songs.

ANY OCCASION

Refrain

Oh, lift me up, and I shall be By faith in heaven eternally, A higher plane than I have found, Oh, plant me, God, on higher ground.

ANY OCCASION

143 When We All Get to Heaven

HEAVEN 8.7.8.7 with Refrain

Eliza E Hewitt (1851–1920)   Emily D. Wilson (1865–1942)

1. Sing the wondrous love of Jesus, Sing His mercy and His grace; In the mansions bright and blessed He'll prepare for us a place.
2. While we walk the pilgrim pathway Clouds will overspread the sky; But when traveling days are over Not a shadow, not a sigh.
3. Let us then be true and faithful, Trusting, serving every day; Just one glimpse of Him in glory Will the toils of life repay.
4. Onward to the prize before us! Soon His beauty we'll behold; Soon the pearly gates will open, We shall tread the streets of gold.

Refrain
When we all get to heav - en, What a day of re-
(When we all) (What a)
joic - ing that will be! When we all see
(day of re - joic - ing that will be!) (When we all)
Je - sus, We'll sing and shout the vic - to - ry.
(shout, and shout the vic - to - ry.)

ANY OCCASION

144 Nobody Knows the Trouble I See

DUBOIS Irr. with Refrain

African-American spiritual

African-American spiritual
adapt. and arr. by William Farley Smith, 1986

Refrain
No-bod-y knows the trou-ble I see, No-bod-y knows but Je-sus;
Oh, no-bod-y knows the trou-ble I see, Glo-ry hal-le-lu-jah! *Fine*

1. Some-times I'm up, some-times I'm down,
2. Al-though you see me going 'long so, Oh, yes, Lord!
3. What makes old Sa-tan hate me so?

Some-times I'm al-most to the ground,
I have my trou-bles here be-low, Oh, yes, Lord! Oh,
'Cause he got me once and let me go,

D.C.

Music: arr. © 1989 The United Methodist Publishing House (Administered By The Copyright Company c/o The Copyright Company, Nashville, TN) All rights reserved. International copyright secured. Used by permission.

ANY OCCASION

Rock of Ages, Cleft for Me

145

TOPLADY 7.7.7.7.7.7

Augustus M. Toplady, 1776 — Thomas Hastings, 1830

1. Rock of Ages, cleft for me, Let me hide myself in Thee; Let the water and the blood, From Thy wounded side which flowed, Be of sin the double cure; Save from wrath and make me pure.

2. Not the labors of my hands Can fulfill Thy law's demands; Could my zeal no respite know, Could my tears forever flow, All for sin could not atone; Thou must save, and Thou alone.

3. Nothing in my hand I bring, Simply to the cross I cling; Naked, come to Thee for dress; Helpless, look to Thee for grace; Foul, I to the fountain fly; Wash me, Savior, or I die.

4. While I draw this fleeting breath, When mine eyes shall close in death, When I soar to worlds unknown, See Thee on Thy judgment throne, Rock of Ages, cleft for me, Let me hide myself in Thee.

ANY OCCASION

146 Softly and Tenderly Jesus Is Calling
THOMPSON 11.7.11.7 with Refrain

Will L. Thompson, 1880 — Will L. Thompson, 1880

1. Soft-ly and ten-der-ly Jesus is call-ing,
   Call-ing for you and for me;
   See, on the por-tals he's wait-ing and watch-ing,
   Watch-ing for you and for me.

2. Why should we tar-ry when Jesus is plead-ing,
   Plead-ing for you and for me?
   Why should we lin-ger and heed not His mer-cies,
   Mer-cies for you and for me?

3. Time is now fleet-ing, the mo-ments are pass-ing,
   Pass-ing from you and from me;
   Shad-ows are gath-er-ing, death-beds are com-ing,
   Com-ing for you and for me.

4. Oh, for the won-der-ful love He has prom-ised,
   Prom-ised for you and for me!
   Though we have sinned, He has mer-cy and par-don,
   Par-don for you and for me.

Refrain
Come home, come home;
(Come home,) (come home;)
You who are

ANY OCCASION

weary, come home; Earnestly, tenderly, Jesus is calling, Calling, "O sinner, come home!"

ANY OCCASION

147 Stand Up, Stand Up for Jesus
WEBB 7.6.7.6.D

George Duffield, Jr., 1858 (Eph. 6:10–17)   George J. Webb, 1830

1. Stand up, stand up for Jesus, ye soldiers of the cross;
2. Stand up, stand up for Jesus, the trumpet call obey;
3. Stand up, stand up for Jesus, stand in His strength alone;
4. Stand up, stand up for Jesus, the strife will not be long;

Lift high His royal banner; it must not suffer loss.
Forth to the mighty conflict in this His glorious day.
The arm of flesh will fail you, ye dare not trust your own.
This day the noise of battle, the next the victor's song.

From victory unto victory His army shall He lead,
Ye that are brave now serve Him against unnumbered foes;
Put on the gospel armor, each piece put on with prayer;
To those who vanquish evil a crown of life shall be;

Till every foe is vanquished and Christ is Lord indeed.
Let courage rise with danger and strength to strength oppose.
Where duty calls or danger, be never wanting there.
They with the King of Glory shall reign eternally.

ANY OCCASION

We Are Climbing Jacob's Ladder   148
JACOB'S LADDER Irregular

African-American spiritual (Gen. 28:10-17)
African-American adapt. and arr. by William Farley Smith, 1986

1. We are climbing Jacob's ladder; We are climbing Jacob's ladder, We are climbing Jacob's ladder;
2. Every round goes higher, higher; Every round goes higher, higher; Every round goes higher, higher;
3. Sinner, do you love my Jesus? Sinner, do you love my Jesus? Sinner, do you love my Jesus?
4. If you love Him, why not serve Him? If you love Him, why not serve Him? If you love Him, why not serve Him?
5. We are climbing higher, higher; We are climbing higher, higher; We are climbing higher, higher;

(yes, Lord;)

(yes, Lord;)

Soldiers of the cross.

Music: arr. © 1989 The United Methodist Publishing House (Administered by The Copyright Company c/o The Copyright Company, Nashville, TN) All rights reserved. International copyright secured. Used by permission.

ANY OCCASION

149   Standing on the Promises
PROMISES 11.11.11.9 with Refrain

R. Kelso Carter, 1886 (Eph. 6:14-17)   R. Kelso Carter, 1886

1.   of Christ my King,
2. Stand-ing on the prom-is-es that can-not fail,
3.   of Christ the Lord,
4.   I can-not fail,

Through e-ter-nal a-ges let His prais-es ring;
When the howl-ing storms of doubt and fear as-sail,
Bound to Him e-ter-nal-ly by love's strong cord,
Lis-tening ev-ery mo-ment to the Spir-it's call,

Glo-ry in the high-est, I will shout and sing,
By the liv-ing Word of God I shall pre-vail,
O-ver-com-ing dai-ly with the Spir-it's sword,
Rest-ing in my Sav-ior as my all in all,

Stand-ing on the prom-is-es of God.

Refrain
Stand - ing, stand - ing,
(Stand - ing on the prom - is - es, stand - ing on the prom - is - es,)
Stand - ing on the prom - is - es of God my Sav - ior;
Stand - ing, stand - ing,
(Stand - ing on the prom - is - es, stand - ing on the prom - is - es,)
I'm stand - ing on the prom - is - es of God.

ANY OCCASION

150 It Is Well with My Soul
VILLE DU HAVRE 11.8.11.9 with Refrain

Horatio G. Spafford, 1873 — Phillip P. Bliss, 1876

1. When peace, like a riv-er, at-tend-eth my way,
2. Though Sa-tan should buf-fet, though tri-als should come,
3. My sin, oh, the bliss of this glo-ri-ous thought!
4. And, Lord, haste the day when my faith shall be sight,

When sor-rows like sea-bil-lows roll; What-ev-er my
Let this blest as-sur-ance con-trol, That Christ has re-
My sin, not in part but the whole, Is nailed to the
The clouds be rolled back as a scroll; The trump shall re-

lot, Thou hast taught me to say, "It is well, it is
gard-ed my help-less es-tate, And hath shed His own
cross, and I bear it no more; Praise the Lord, praise the
sound, and the Lord shall de-scend, E-ven so, it is

ANY OCCASION

well   with   my   soul."
blood   for   my   soul.
Lord,   O   my   soul!   It is well   with my
well   with   my   soul.   (It is well)

soul, _____ It is well, it is well with my soul.
(with my soul,)

ANY OCCASION

151 Sweet Hour of Prayer
SWEET HOUR L.M.D

William Walford, 1845 — William B. Bradbury, 1861

1. That calls me from a world of care And bids me at my Father's throne Make all my wants and wishes known: In seasons of distress and grief, My soul has
2. Sweet hour of prayer! sweet hour of prayer! The joys I feel, the bliss I share Of those whose anxious spirits burn With strong desires for thy return! With such I hasten to the place Where God my
3. Thy wings shall my petition bear To Him Whose truth and faithfulness Engage the waiting soul to bless. And since He bids me seek His face, Believe His

ANY OCCASION

of - ten found re - lief, And oft es - caped the tempt - er's snare By thy re - turn,
Sav - ior shows His face, And glad - ly take my sta - tion there, And wait for thee, sweet hour of prayer!
word, and trust His grace, I'll cast on Him my ev - ery care, And wait for thee,

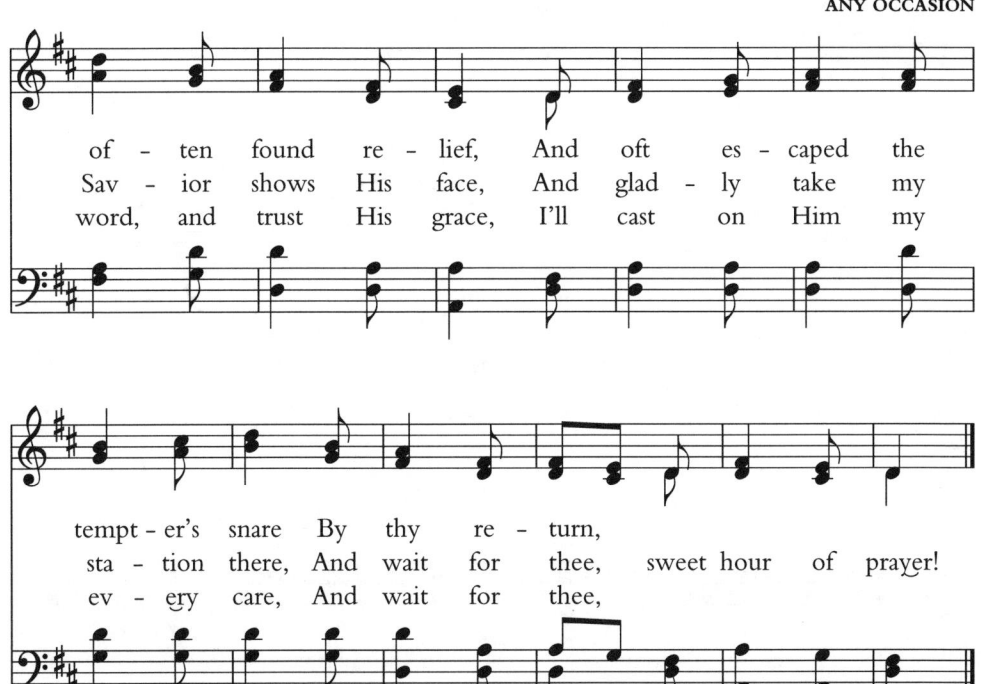

ANY OCCASION

152 Jesus, Savior, Pilot Me
PILOT 7.7.7.7.7.7

Edward Hopper, 1871
(Mt. 8:23–27; Mk. 4:35–41; Lk. 8:22–25)

John E. Gould, 1871

1. Jesus, Savior, pilot me Over life's tempestuous sea; Unknown waves before me roll, Hiding rock and treacherous shoal. Chart and compass came from Thee; Jesus, Savior, pilot me.

2. As a mother stills her child, Thou canst hush the ocean wild; Boisterous waves obey Thy will, When Thou sayest to them, "Be still!" Wondrous sovereign of the sea, Jesus, Savior, pilot me.

3. When at last I near the shore, And the fearful breakers roar 'Twixt me and the peaceful rest, Then, while leaning on Thy breast, May I hear Thee say to me, "Fear not, I will pilot thee."

ANY OCCASION

Come, Ye Disconsolate
153
CONSOLATOR 11.10.11.10

Thomas Moore, 1816
alt. by Thomas Hastings, 1831

Samuel Webbe, Sr., 1792

1. Come, ye dis-con-so-late, wher-e'er ye lan-guish,
   Come to the mer-cy seat, fer-vent-ly kneel.
   Here bring your wound-ed hearts, here tell your an-guish;
   Earth has no sor-row that heaven can-not heal.

2. Joy of the des-o-late, Light of the stray-ing,
   Hope of the pen-i-tent, fade-less and pure!
   Here speaks the Com-fort-er, ten-der-ly say-ing,
   "Earth has no sor-row that heaven can-not cure."

3. Here see the Bread of Life; see waters flow-ing
   Forth from the throne of God, pure from a-bove.
   Come to the feast of love; come, ev-er know-ing
   Earth has no sor-row but heaven can re-move.

ANY OCCASION

154 Leaning on the Everlasting Arms
SHOWALTER 10.9.10.9 with Refrain

Elisha A. Hoffman, 1887 (Dt. 33:27) Anthony J. Showalter, 1887

1. What a fel-low-ship, what a joy di-vine, Leaning on the ev-er-last-ing arms; What a bless-ed-ness, what a peace is mine,
2. Oh, how sweet to walk in this pil-grim way, Leaning on the ev-er-last-ing arms; Oh, how bright the path grows from day to day,
3. What have I to dread, what have I to fear, Leaning on the ev-er-last-ing arms? I have bless-ed peace with my Lord so near,

Refrain

Lean-ing on the ev-er-last-ing arms. Lean - ing, lean - ing, Safe and se-cure from all a-larms; Lean -
(Lean-ing on Je-sus,) (lean-ing on Je-sus,) (Lean-ing on)

ing, lean - ing, Lean-ing on the ev-er-last-ing arms.
(Je - sus, lean - ing on Je - sus,)

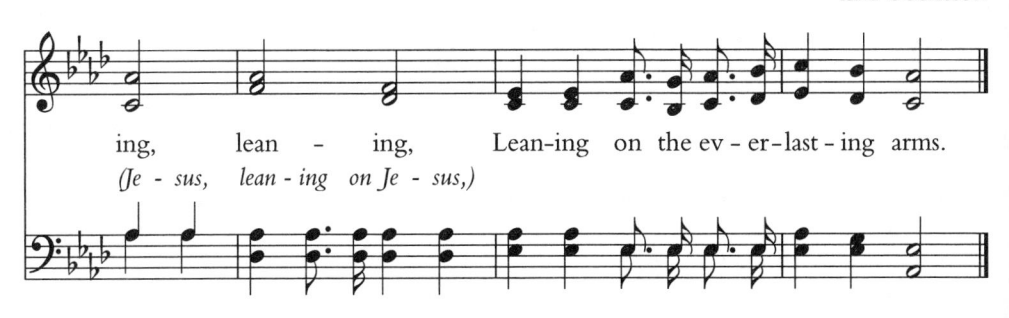

Must Jesus Bear the Cross Alone 155
MAITLAND C.M.

Thomas Shepherd and others, 1855
George N. Allen, 1844

1. Must Je - sus bear the cross a - lone, and all the world go free? No, there's a cross for ev - ery - one, and there's a cross for me.
2. How hap - py are the saints a - bove, who once went sor - row-ing here! But now they taste un - min - gled love and joy with-out a tear.
3. The con - se - crat - ed cross I'll bear till death shall set me free; And then go home my crown to wear, for there's a crown for me.

ANY OCCASION

ANY OCCASION

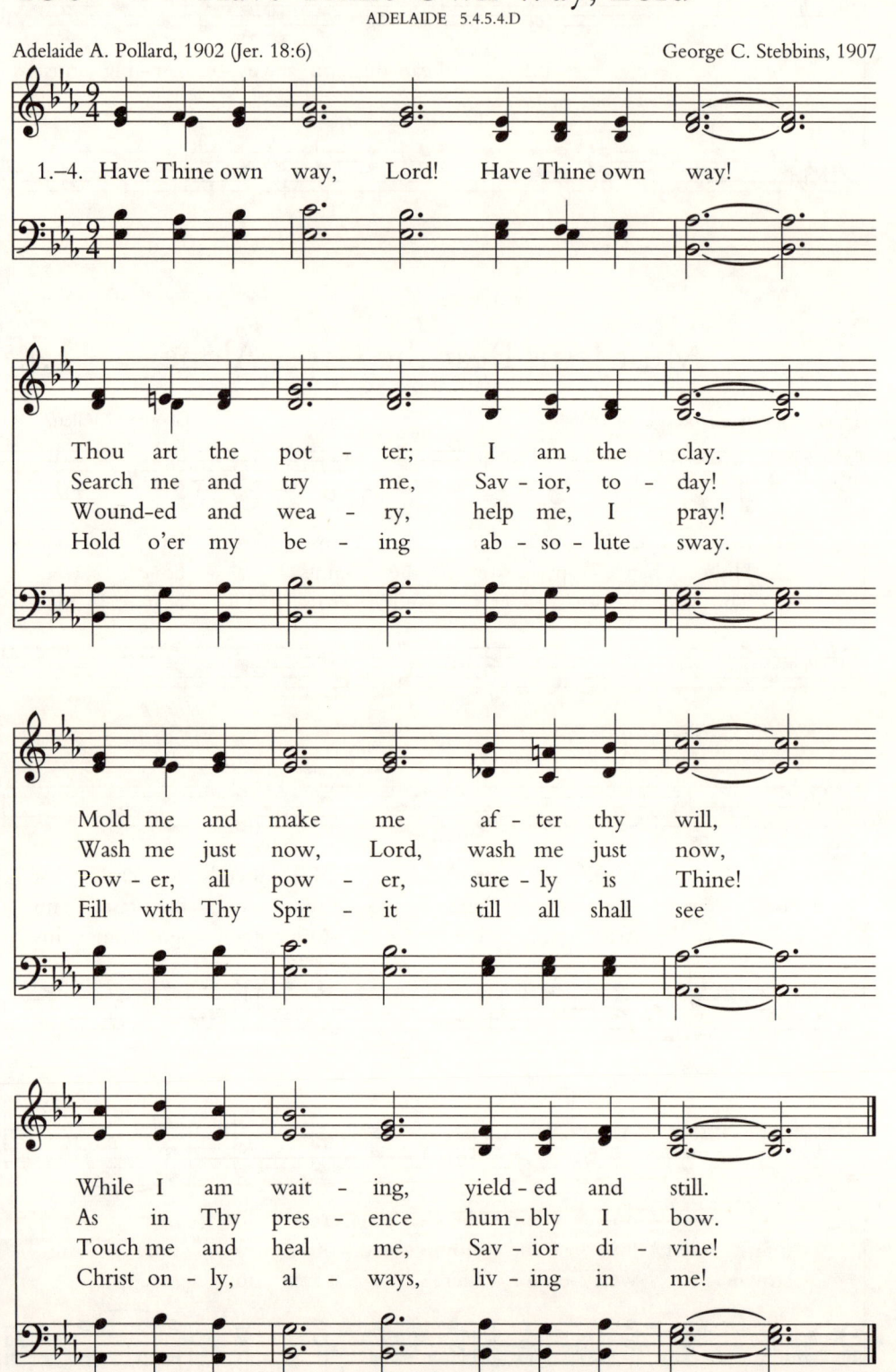

156 Have Thine Own Way, Lord
ADELAIDE 5.4.5.4.D

Adelaide A. Pollard, 1902 (Jer. 18:6)　　　　　　　　　　　George C. Stebbins, 1907

1.–4. Have Thine own way, Lord! Have Thine own way!

Thou art the pot - ter; I am the clay.
Search me and try me, Sav - ior, to - day!
Wound-ed and wea - ry, help me, I pray!
Hold o'er my be - ing ab - so - lute sway.

Mold me and make me af - ter thy will,
Wash me just now, Lord, wash me just now,
Pow - er, all pow - er, sure - ly is Thine!
Fill with Thy Spir - it till all shall see

While I am wait - ing, yield - ed and still.
As in Thy pres - ence hum - bly I bow.
Touch me and heal me, Sav - ior di - vine!
Christ on - ly, al - ways, liv - ing in me!

ANY OCCASION

I Need Thee Every Hour

157

NEED 6.4.6.4 with Refrain

Annie S. Hawks, 1872 (Jn. 15:5) — Robert Lowry, 1873

1.
2.
3. I need Thee ev-ery hour, in joy or pain;
4.
5.

1. most gracious Lord;
2. stay Thou near - by;
3.
4. teach me Thy will;
5. most Ho - ly One;

No ten - der voice like Thine can peace af - ford.
Temp - ta - tions lose their power when Thou art nigh.
Come quick - ly and a - bide, or life is vain.
And Thy rich prom - is - es in me ful - fill.
Oh, make me Thine in - deed, Thou bless - ed Son.

Refrain

I need Thee, Oh, I need Thee; ev - ery hour I need Thee;
Oh, bless me now, my Sav - ior, I come to Thee.

ANY OCCASION

158   I Am Thine, O Lord
I AM THINE   10.7.10.7 with Refrain

Fanny J. Crosby, 1875 (Heb. 10:22)   William H. Doane, 1875

1. I am Thine, O Lord, I have heard Thy voice, And it told Thy love to me; But I long to rise in the arms of faith And be clos-er drawn to Thee.
2. Con-se-crate me now to Thy ser-vice, Lord, By the power of grace di-vine; Let my soul look up with a stead-fast hope, And my will be lost in Thine.
3. Oh, the pure de-light of a sin-gle hour That be-fore Thy throne I spend, When I kneel in prayer, and with Thee, my God, I com-mune as friend with friend!
4. There are depths of love that I can-not know Till I cross the nar-row sea; There are heights of joy that I may not reach Till I rest in peace with Thee.

ANY OCCASION

Refrain

Draw me near - er, near-er, bless-ed Lord, To the
(near - er, near - er,)
cross where Thou hast died. Draw me near - er, near - er,
near - er, bless-ed Lord, To Thy pre - cious, bleed-ing side.

ANY OCCASION

159 Trust and Obey

TRUST AND OBEY 6.6.9.D with Refrain

John H. Sammis, 1887 (1 Jn. 1:7) — Daniel B. Towner, 1887

1. When we walk with the Lord in the light of His Word,
2. Not a bur-den we bear, not a sor-row we share,
3. But we nev-er can prove the de-lights of His love
4. Then in fel-low-ship sweet we will sit at His feet,

What a glo-ry He sheds on our way!
But our toil He doth rich-ly re-pay;
Un-til all on the al-tar we lay;
Or we'll walk by His side in the way;

While we do His good will, He a-bides with us still,
Not a grief or a loss, not a frown or a cross,
For the fa-vor He shows, for the joy He be-stows,
What He says we will do, where He sends we will go;

And with all who will trust and o-bey.
But is blest if we trust and o-bey.
Are for them who will trust and o-bey.
Nev-er fear, on-ly trust and o-bey.

ANY OCCASION

Refrain

Trust and o-bey, For there's no oth-er way To be hap-py in Je-sus, But to trust and o-bey.

ANY OCCASION

160 Shall We Gather at the River
HANSON PLACE 8.7.8.7 with Refrain

Robert Lowry, 1864 (Rev. 22:1–5)   Robert Lowry, 1864

1. Shall we gather at the river, Where bright angel feet have trod, With its crystal tide forever Flowing by the throne of God?
2. On the margin of the river, Washing up its silver spray, We will walk and worship ever, All the happy golden day.
3. Ere we reach the shining river, Lay we every burden down; Grace our spirits will deliver, And provide a robe and crown.
4. Soon we'll reach the shining river, Soon our pilgrimage will cease; Soon our happy hearts will quiver With the melody of peace.

Refrain
Yes, we'll gather at the river, The beautiful, the beautiful river; Gather with the

ANY OCCASION

saints at the river That flows by the throne of God.

Come, We That Love the Lord 161
ST. THOMAS S.M.

Isaac Watts, 1707

Aaron Williams,
The New Universal Psalmodist, 1770

1. Come, we that love the Lord, And let our joys be known; Join in a song with sweet accord, And thus surround the throne.
2. Let those refuse to sing Who never knew our God; But children of the heavenly King May speak their joys abroad.
3. The hill of Zion yields A thousand sacred sweets Before we reach the heavenly fields Or walk the golden streets.
4. Then let our songs abound, And every tear be dry; We're marching through Emmanuel's ground, To fairer worlds on high.

ANY OCCASION

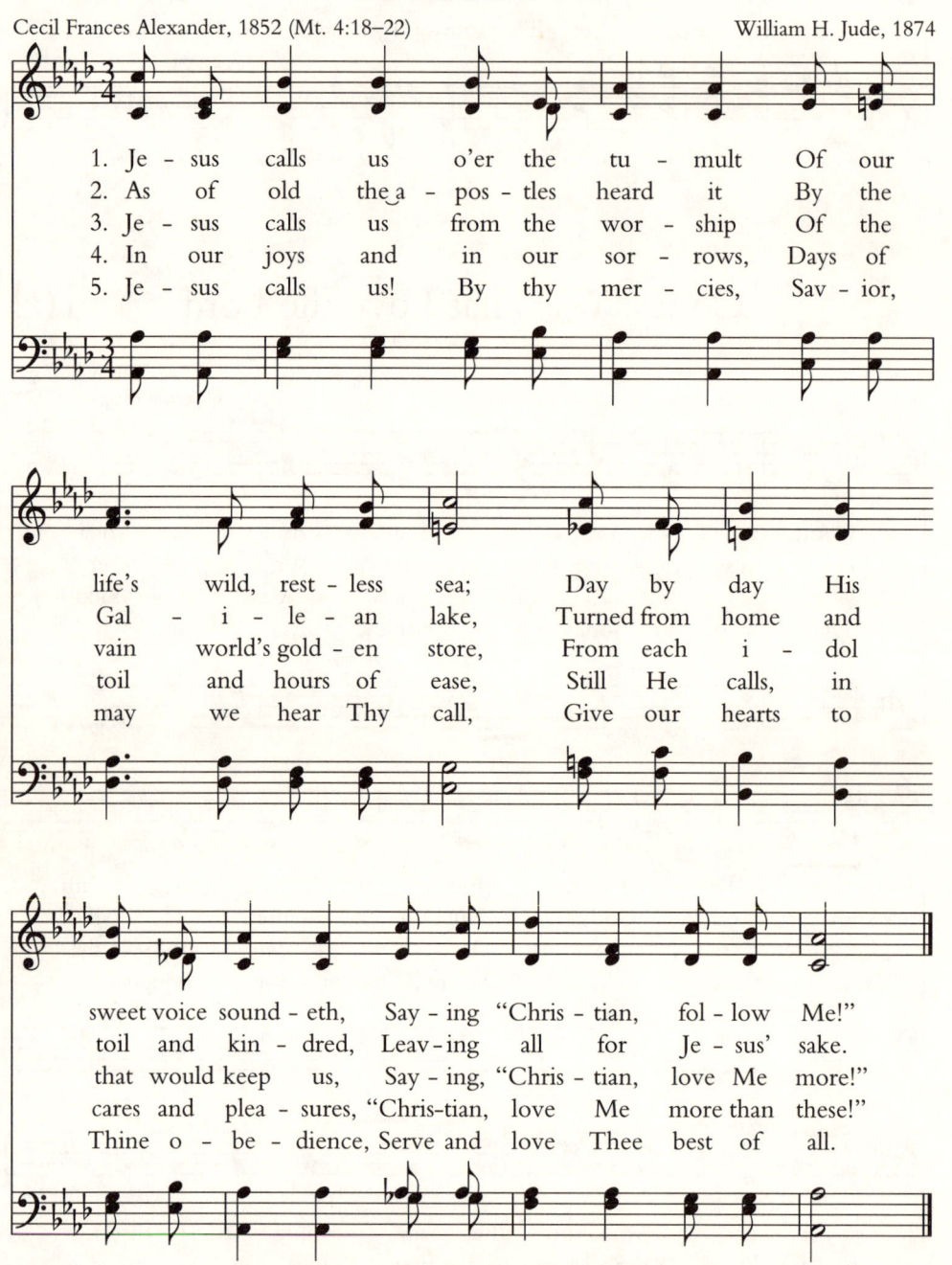

162 Jesus Calls Us
GALILEE 8.7.8.7

Cecil Frances Alexander, 1852 (Mt. 4:18–22) William H. Jude, 1874

1. Jesus calls us o'er the tumult Of our life's wild, restless sea; Day by day His sweet voice sound-eth, Saying "Christian, follow Me!"
2. As of old the apostles heard it By the Galilean lake, Turned from home and toil and kindred, Leaving all for Jesus' sake.
3. Jesus calls us from the worship Of the vain world's golden store, From each idol that would keep us, Saying, "Christian, love Me more!"
4. In our joys and in our sorrows, Days of toil and hours of ease, Still He calls, in cares and pleasures, "Christian, love Me more than these!"
5. Jesus calls us! By thy mercies, Savior, may we hear Thy call, Give our hearts to Thine obedience, Serve and love Thee best of all.

INDEX OF FIRST LINES AND COMMON TITLES

Abide with Me 112
Ah, Holy Jesus 9
All Hail the Power of Jesus' Name! 14
All to Jesus I Surrender (I Surrender All) ... 131
Amazing Grace, How Sweet the Sound 24
Amen, Amen 32
Are Ye Able 132
As with Gladness Men of Old 5
Ask Ye What Great Thing I Know 28
Be Not Dismayed (God Will Take
  Care of You) 20
Be Thou My Vision 55
Beneath the Cross of Jesus 8
Blessed Assurance, Jesus is Mine 58
Blest Be the Tie That Binds 89
Break Thou the Bread of Life 51
Breathe on Me, Breath of God 47
Bringing in the Sheaves (Sowing
  in the Morning) 141
Come, Christians, Join to Sing 15
Come, Thou Almighty King 13
Come, Thou Font of Every Blessing 64
Come, We That Love the Lord 161
Come, Ye Disconsolate 153
Count Your Blessings 120
Dear Lord and Father of Mankind 57
Down at the Cross 7
Every Time I Feel the Spirit 46
Fairest Lord Jesus 40
Faith Is the Victory 121
For All the Saints 108
Give Me Jesus 127
Go Tell It on the Mountain 2
God Moves in a Mysterious Way 18
God of Grace and God of Glory 87
Great Day! 92
Great Is Thy Faithfulness 22
Guide Me, O Thou Great Jehovah 25
Guide My Feet 63
Have Thine Own Way, Lord 156
He Leadeth Me: O Blessed Thought 19
He Lives 37
Here I Am, Lord 106
Here, O Lord, We See You Face to Face ... 105
Holy, Holy, Holy, Lord God Almighty! 12
How Firm a Foundation 67
How Great Thou Art 96
I Am Thine, O Lord 158
I Come to the Garden Alone
  (In the Garden) 36
I Danced in the Morning 39
I Greet Thee Who My Sure Redeemer Art .. 97
I Have Decided to Follow Jesus 84
I Have Found a Friend in Jesus (The Lily
  of the Valley) 34
I Know the Lord's Laid His Hands on Me ... 62

I Love to Tell the Story 31
I Need Thee Every Hour 157
I Sing the Mighty Power of God 27
I Would Be True 139
If Thou But Trust in God to Guide Thee ... 26
I'm Gonna Live So God Can Use Me 68
I'm Pressing on the Upward Way (Higher
  Ground) 142
Immortal, Invisible, God Only Wise 21
Immortal Love, Forever Full 30
It is Well with My Soul 150
I've Wandered Far Away from God 134
Jesus Calls Us 162
Jesus Is Tenderly Calling Thee Home 54
Jesus Keep Me near the Cross 35
Jesus Paid It All (I Hear the Savior Say) 136
Jesus, Savior, Pilot Me 152
Jesus, the Very Thought of Thee 44
Jesus Walked This Lonesome Valley 6
Just A Closer Walk with Thee 86
Just As I Am, without One Plea 69
Lead, Kindly Light 56
Lead, On, O King Eternal 93
Leaning on the Everlasting Arms 154
Let the Lower Lights Be Burning (Brightly
  Beams Our Father's Mercy) 135
Let Us Break Bread Together 103
Lift Up Your Heads, Ye Mighty Gates 1
Living for Jesus a Life That Is True 83
Lo, How a Rose E'er Blooming 3
Lord, I Want to Be a Christian 70
Lord, Speak to Me, That I May Speak 130
Love Divine, All Loves Excelling 72
Love Lifted Me (I Was Sinking Deep
  in Sin) 137
Low in the Grave He Lay (Up from the
  Grave He Arose) 38
Master, No Offering Costly and Sweet 53
More Love to Thee, O Christ 66
Morning Has Broken 98
Must Jesus Bear the Cross Alone 155
My Faith Looks Up to Thee 74
My Hope Is Built on Nothing Less 71
My Jesus, I Love Thee 81
My Lord! What a Morning 94
My Soul in Sad Exile (The Haven of Rest) .. 140
Near to the Heart of God 109
Nearer My God to Thee 133
Nobody Knows the Trouble I See 144
O God of Bethel, by Whose Hand 23
O Jesus, I Have Promised 61
O Love That Wilt Not Let Me Go 75
O Master, Let Me Walk With Thee 65
O Safe to the Rock (Hiding in Thee) 114
O Word of God Incarnate 50
Of the Father's Love Begotten 43

Oh, How I Love Jesus 33
Once to Every Man and Nation 60
Open My Eyes, That I May See 48
Out of My Bondage, Sorrow, and Night ... 113
Pass Me Not, O Gentle Savior 138
Praise Him, All Ye Little Children 123
Praise Him! Praise Him! 41
Praise My Soul, the King of Heaven 99
Praise Ye the Lord, the Almighty 95
Precious Lord, Take My Hand 79
Redeemed, How I Love to Proclaim It 119
Rejoice, the Lord Is King 16
Rescue the Perishing 88
Rise Up, Shepherd, and Follow 4
Rock of Ages, Cleft for Me 145
Savior, Like a Shepherd Lead Us 76
Send the Light 118
Shall We Gather at the River 160
Sing Them Over Again to Me (Wonderful
 Words of Life) 52
Softly and Tenderly Jesus Is Calling 146
Somebody's Knocking at Your Door 73
Spirit of God, Descend upon My Heart 49
Stand Up, Stand Up for Jesus 147
Standing on the Promises 149
Steal Away to Jesus 124
Sunshine in My Soul 122
Sweet By and By (There's a Land That is
 Fairer Than Day) 110
Sweet Hour of Prayer 151
Swing Low, Sweet Chariot 111

Take My Life 77
Take the Name of Jesus with You (Precious
 Name) 126
Take Time to Be Holy 128
Tell Me the Stories of Jesus 41
Ten Thousand Times Ten Thousand 82
The Church's One Foundation 91
The Great Physician 116
The Lord's My Shepherd, I'll Not Want 17
There Is a Balm in Gilead 18
There Is a Fountain Filled with Blood 104
There Is a Green Hill Far Away 29
There Is Power in the Blood 45
There Shall Be Showers of Blessing 125
'Tis So Sweet to Trust in Jesus 129
To God Be the Glory 102
True-Hearted, Whole-Hearted 117
Trust and Obey 159
We Are Climbing Jacob's Ladder 148
We Would See Jesus 85
Were You There? 11
We've a Story to Tell to the Nations 90
What a Friend We Have in Jesus 80
When I Survey the Wondrous Cross 10
When Morning Gilds the Skies 101
When the Roll is Called up Yonder (When
 the Trumpet of the Lord) 107
When We All Get to Heaven 143
Who Is on the Lord's Side? 59
Ye Servants of God, Your Master Proclaim .. 100
Yield Not to Temptation 115